# GALLUP
## MAJOR TRENDS & EVENTS
### The Pulse of Our Nation: 1900 to the Present

# Drug & Alcohol Abuse

# GALLUP
## MAJOR TRENDS & EVENTS
### The Pulse of Our Nation: 1900 to the Present

**Abortion**

**Drug & Alcohol Abuse**

**Health Care**

**Immigration**

**Marriage & Family Issues**

**Obesity**

**Race Relations**

**Technology**

# GALLUP
## MAJOR TRENDS & EVENTS
### *The Pulse of Our Nation: 1900 to the Present*

# Drug & Alcohol Abuse

## Hal Marcovitz

Produced by OTTN Publishing, Stockton, New Jersey

Mason Crest Publishers
370 Reed Road
Broomall, PA 19008
www.masoncrest.com

Library of Congress Cataloging-in-Publication Data

Marcovitz, Hal.
  Drugs and alcohol / Hal Marcovitz.
     p. cm. — (Gallup major trends and events)
  Includes bibliographical references and index.
  ISBN-13: 978-1-59084-963-7 (hard cover)
  ISBN-10: 1-59084-963-9 (hard cover)
  1. Drug abuse—United States—Juvenile literature. 2. Alcoholism—United
States—Juvenile literature. I. Title. II. Series.
  HV5809.5.M333 2005
  362.29—dc22
                            2005016302

# TABLE OF CONTENTS

# 1 ALCOHOL AND DRUGS IN AMERICA

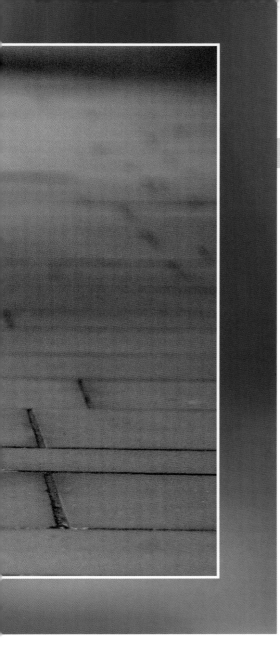

This woman has passed out after consuming too much alcohol. A 2003 survey suggests that 54 million Americans—more than 17 percent of the total U.S. population—have engaged in episodes of dangerous "binge" drinking.

Today, abuse of alcohol and drugs is a significant issue in American society. Substance abuse does not just cause physical and psychological harm to the user, it also contributes to many social problems, such as higher crime and family breakups. Statistics indicate that despite efforts by government and social service agencies to educate Americans about the dangers of drug and alcohol abuse, the problem continues to grow.

## THE PROBLEM OF ALCOHOL ABUSE

Alcohol use is widespread in the United States. According to a 2003 National Survey on Drug Use and Health conducted by the U.S. Substance Abuse and Mental Health Services Administration (SAMHSA), 119 million Americans age 12 and over—about half of the total U.S. population in that category—ingested alcoholic beverages in 2003. SAMHSA also reported that about 54 million Americans participated in episodes of binge drinking at least once in the 30 days prior to the survey.

The Gallup Organization, a company that conducts scientific polls on questions of national interest, has been asking Americans about their drinking habits for some 60 years. In 2005, a Gallup poll determined that 21 percent of Americans admit to drinking "more than they should." In addition, 30 percent of Americans told a Gallup poll in 1997 that drinking has caused problems in their families. In 1947, when the Gallup poll first posed that question, just 15 percent of respondents said drinking had caused problems in their families.

There is no question that drinking causes many problems, and not just in the family. People who drink and drive have accidents that often result in property damage, injury, and death. The National Academies, an organization of science and medical research groups, estimate that underage drinking alone costs Americans some $53 billion a year. People who drink heavily often develop medical problems that could shorten their lives by years. Many organs can be affected by drinking, including the heart, stomach, lungs, liver, brain, and esophagus. Pregnant women who drink can subject their babies to fetal alcohol syndrome — a condition that could cause miscarriages or, if the baby is carried to term, mental retardation, stunted growth, heart and bladder disease, and other birth defects.

"There were nearly 20,000 alcohol-induced deaths in 2001, the last year for which data are available from the National Center for Health Statistics," says a 2004 Gallup analysis. "And these numbers do not include deaths from unintentional injuries or homicides, many of which may indirectly be related to alcohol use. Alcohol consumption is clearly a major health risk factor."

A Gallup poll taken in 2004 reported 23 percent of men and 38 percent of women had not taken a drink of alcohol within seven days of the survey, yet 52 percent of men and 53 percent of women had consumed up to seven drinks in the week prior to the survey. In addition, 14 percent of men and 5 percent of women said they had consumed as many as 19 drinks in the week prior to the survey, and 9 percent of men and 2 percent of women admitted to consuming 20 or more drinks in the week prior to the survey. Said the Gallup analysis:

> Occasional drinking does not necessarily indicate a drinking problem, but even small amounts of alcohol can cause slurred speech, slowed reaction times, or impaired judgment. The Centers for Disease Control and Prevention defines "excessive drinking" as an average of

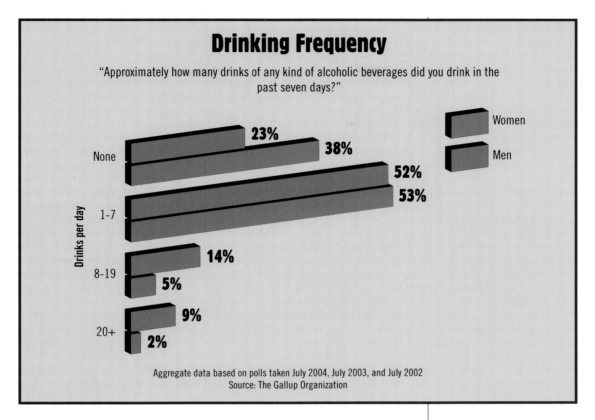

## Drinking Frequency

"Approximately how many drinks of any kind of alcoholic beverages did you drink in the past seven days?"

Women
Men

None — 23% / 38%

1-7 — 52% / 53%

8-19 — 14% / 5%

20+ — 9% / 2%

Drinks per day

Aggregate data based on polls taken July 2004, July 2003, and July 2002
Source: The Gallup Organization

more than one drink per day for women, and an average of more than two drinks per day for men. . . . Objective measures of how many drinks one has in a week can only go so far in defining problems with alcohol. Regardless of how much a person drinks, alcohol consumption is a problem if it negatively affects the way the person thinks, feels, or interacts with others.

## THE DANGER OF DRUG ADDICTION

Fewer Americans abuse drugs than drink alcohol. SAMHSA's 2003 National Survey on Drug Use and Health estimated that 19.5 million Americans—8.2 percent of the population age 12 and older—are current users of illicit drugs. However, the cost of drug use to society, as well as to the users and their families, is just as severe.

Although a "war on drugs" has been waged in the United States for decades, drug abuse remains a problem throughout the country. Each year, Congress appropriates some $2 billion to the U.S. Drug Enforcement Administration (DEA) to combat illegal drugs. Other agencies, such as the Federal Bureau of Investigation (FBI), Coast Guard, and Customs Service, devote significant resources to the drug war as well. And state and local governments spend millions of dollars a year on their own efforts to break up drug rings and imprison those responsible for dealing the drugs. But those efforts have proven unable to stop the flow of illegally smuggled cocaine, marijuana, or heroin into the United States, or wipe out the drug laboratories hidden in basements and garages.

"Americans spend approximately $65 billion per year on illicit drugs, but the costs to society from drug consumption far exceed this amount," says DEA administrator Karen P. Tandy. Speaking before the U.S. House of Representatives Committee on Appropriations in March of 2004, Tandy explained, "Illegal drugs cost the economy $98.5 billion in lost earnings, $12.9 billion in health care costs, and $32.1 billion in other costs, including social welfare costs and the cost

DEA agents destroy bundles of illegal cocaine seized in a drug raid.

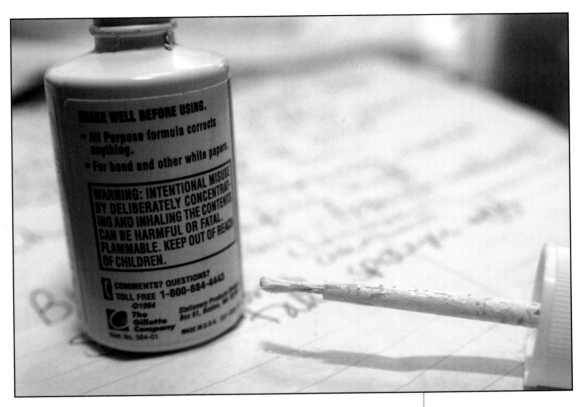

of goods and services lost to crime. Current seizures of drug proceeds by all law enforcement combined are estimated at $1 billion per year—less than 1 percent of the illicit drug market."

And those numbers do not tell the whole story. The DEA and other law enforcement agencies are not well equipped to police the use of inhalants—ordinary household products such as glue, gasoline, and computer cleaner that can provide a quick and cheap high when sniffed. Also, one of the newest trends in drug abuse finds young people reaching into the medicine cabinets at home and swallowing the prescription painkillers obtained by their parents. Inhalant products and prescription painkillers are both obtained through legal means, so authorities find it quite difficult to keep them out of the hands of substance abusers.

While the government's ongoing "war on drugs" focuses on such illegal substances as heroin, cocaine, and marijuana, young people are also using some common household products, such as liquid correction fluid, to get high. It is difficult to monitor inhalant abuse because most of these products can be obtained legally.

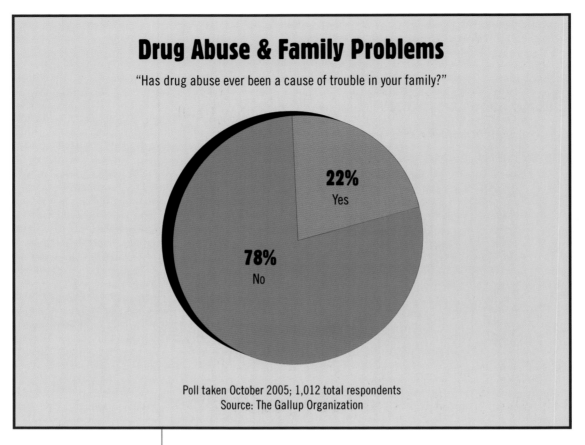

# Drug Abuse & Family Problems

"Has drug abuse ever been a cause of trouble in your family?"

22%
Yes

78%
No

Poll taken October 2005; 1,012 total respondents
Source: The Gallup Organization

Drugs cause as many health problems as alcohol. Depending on the drug of choice, the heart, brain, and other organs, can be permanently affected, as can the central nervous system, muscles, skin, and bones. Drug users risk mental illness as well as a host of physical problems. Accidental and overdose deaths among drug users are common.

As with alcohol, many Americans are troubled by the issue of drug abuse. A 2005 Gallup poll reported that 22 percent of Americans believe drug abuse has caused problems in their families. And according to another Gallup poll taken earlier in 2005, 42 percent of American adults worry "a great deal" about drug abuse in the United States, while another 23 percent worry "a fair amount." One Massachusetts mother who responded to this 2005 poll commented on her fears. "My own children are fine, but often they tell me about some of their childhood friends who became addicted to drugs," the 74-year-old woman said. "It breaks my heart to hear these stories about children that I still remember as the nicest little kids in the world."

# 2 THE "NOBLE EXPERIMENT" AND BEYOND

Since colonial times, alcohol has been an important part of American life. Among the Founding Fathers, Thomas Jefferson once said that wine was a "necessary of life," while Benjamin Franklin famously remarked, "Beer is living proof that God loves us and wants us to be happy."

Americans have always taken their drinking very seriously. In colonial times, farmers and tradesmen would gather in taverns to sip ale and talk business and politics. The tavern, always located along a main road for easy access to weary travelers, could also serve as a town hall or a courtroom. In the days before most communities had the wherewithal to erect a courthouse in the town square, the village tavern often served as a place where civil disputes could be settled or charges of banditry could be leveled against a local scoundrel.

In 1776, as the founding fathers gathered at the old State House in Philadelphia to draft the Declaration of Independence, many disputes over the wording of the historic document were resolved at the nearby Indian Queen Tavern. As Thomas Jefferson labored over the draft of the document in a room above the tavern, he probably kept a glass of wine within reach. Later, when the Continental Army was sent into the field to face the British, the quartermaster made sure each man was issued a quart of beer along with his other rations.

Following the Revolution, the new secretary of the treasury, Alexander Hamilton, hit upon the idea of raising money for the new government by assessing a tax on distilled liquor. This intrusion by the federal government into the drinking habits of its citizenry caused a 1794 uprising known as the Whiskey Rebellion. Congress was forced to raise an army and send 15,000 soldiers into Western Pennsylvania to put down the revolt. Later, American troops fighting against the British in the War of 1812 were issued rum along with their rations of beef, flour, vinegar, and salt.

By the time of the Civil War (1861–65), coffee had replaced rum in the mess tents, but drinking in the camps remained common. At the same time, a temperance movement was growing in the United States. The so-called "drys" believed drinking was getting out of control. They formed organizations such as the American Temperance Union, Sons of Temperance, and Congressional Temperance Union, drawing their support from the memberships of Protestant churches. Ministers exhorted their flocks to give up drinking. Still, during times of crises like the Civil War, Americans were loathe to give up the bottle.

But the temperance movement would not go away. In 1873, a new group was formed, the Women's Christian Temperance Union (WCTU), and this time, the drys aimed to make their message stick. They focused first on children, hoping to instill in them a belief that drinking is wrong. WCTU leaders convinced the publisher of *McGuffey's Reader*—the most common textbook found in American schoolhouses—to include an anti-saloon message in the books.

In 1884, opposition to drinking surfaced as an issue in the presidential election. Drys defected from the Republican Party, forming their own Prohibition Party. Prohibition candidate John P. St. John earned just 150,000 votes, but he helped deny the presidency to Republican James G. Blaine. The so-called "wets" supported Democrat Grover Cleveland, who won the White House by a razor-thin margin. Despite the loss, Prohibition Party members continued to promote their issue. In the 1892 presidential election, Prohibition candidate John Bidwell received more than 270,000 votes.

Meanwhile, drys lobbied their state legislatures hoping to win adoption of laws banning the sale of alcoholic beverages. These efforts had limited success, as most state legislatures decided to let town and city

NATIONAL PROHIBITION CONVENTION, 1892.

councils decide for themselves whether they wished to adopt anti-drinking ordinances in their municipalities. Clearly, the drys realized, a national campaign was needed to advance their cause.

## GIVING CARRY NATION THE HATCHET

The woman who would become the most famous figure of that campaign was born in 1846 in rural Garrard County, Kentucky. As a young girl, Carry Amelia Moore watched her grandfather get drunk before breakfast every morning. Her first husband, Dr. Charles Gloyd, was also a heavy drinker—he even showed up drunk for their wedding ceremony. Less than a year after they were married, Gloyd dropped dead, evidently from alcohol poisoning. A decade later, in 1877, Carry married again, taking for a husband an itinerant minister named David Nation.

In 1889 the Nations moved to Kansas, and Carry Nation dedicated herself to the temperance movement. While living in Barber County, Kansas, she founded

A large crowd gathers to hear the speakers during the Prohibition Party's 1892 National Convention. That year the party had its best showing, with presidential candidate John Bidwell receiving 271,058 votes (2.3 percent of the total).

Carry Nation, a prominent figure in the temperance movement, gained a reputation as a firebrand by vandalizing saloons. This 1895 cartoon shows a hatchet-wielding Nation menacing a bartender.

and became president of a local chapter of the WCTU. Kansas was a dry state but the law was rarely enforced and every town had a saloon. In the town of Medicine Lodge, Nation led prayer meetings in front of the local tavern — often standing with the other WCTU members right outside the front doors of the saloon. Word quickly spread through Barber County; soon, drys from throughout the county were joining Nation in song and prayer at the saloon doors.

By 1900, Carry Nation had taken her message of temperance onto the road. A typical tactic found her loading a wagon with bricks, stones, and scrap wood and then heaving the debris at the taverns, often striking tipsy drinkers as they emerged from the swinging saloon doors. Eventually, she grew bolder — she would stride into a saloon and hurl rocks at the rows of liquor

bottles lining the shelves behind the bar. In the town of Kiowa, Kansas, she destroyed three saloons before the sheriff caught up with her. According to the book *The Spirits of America: A Social History of Alcohol*, as a crowd gathered round and the sheriff threatened to arrest her, Nation hastily pointed out to the peace officer that drinking was illegal in Kansas. "Men of Kiowa," she proclaimed, "I have destroyed three of your places of business! If I have broken a statute of Kiowa, put me in jail. If I am not a lawbreaker, your Mayor and Councilmen are. You must arrest one of us." She had made her point. The sheriff let her go, and the temperance crusade continued.

Soon, she replaced her bricks and stones with an axe, striding into illegal drinking establishments, from the elegant to the rundown, where she would smash bottles, countertops, stools, and glassware. She was known to proclaim, "God gave Samson the jawbone! He gave David the sling, and he has given Carry Nation the hatchet!"

Nation earned a national reputation and spent the next decade smashing saloons, but she lost a large measure of credibility when she announced that President William F. McKinley, assassinated by an anarchist in 1901, had gotten what he deserved because he was secretly a drinker. She had many other problems later in her life. Her husband divorced her in 1902, claiming her notoriety had ruined his life. Nation's daughter, born from her brief union with Dr. Gloyd, was troubled by mental illness and spent most of her life in institutions. Carry Nation retired from tavern busting in 1910, after she entered a saloon in Montana and was intercepted by the female proprietor who disagreed with her tactics, delivering a sound thrashing to the temperance firebrand. Defeated, Nation went home to Arkansas and died a year later. Etched into her headstone is the epitaph, "She Hath Done What She Could."

## MOVEMENT TOWARD PROHIBITION

Other organizations helped push the temperance cause, such as the Anti-Saloon League, an organization established in 1893. Through the efforts of the Anti-Saloon League, by 1913 nine states had enacted laws outlawing alcohol sales and local anti-drinking ordinances were in effect in 31 other states.

The movement toward a national ban on the sale or use of alcohol—known as Prohibition—was delayed due to the outbreak of World War I. Still, the Anti-Saloon League and other temperance organizations were able to use the war to further their cause. Anti-German sentiment was running high in the United States, particularly after the 1915 sinking of the ocean liner *Lusitania* and the 1917 interception of the Zimmerman Telegram, a secret message from Germany to Mexico encouraging that country to attack the United States. Many Americans shunned German products, changing the German names of streets and towns. Because German families operated many breweries in the United States, some Americans began to associate beer with an evil enemy.

In 1917, Congress passed an amendment to the U.S. Constitution calling for a national ban on the manufacture, sale, transportation, and importation of alcoholic beverages. It took just one year and eight days for the required three-quarters of the states to ratify the amendment. On January 16, 1919, Nebraska became the 36th state to ratify, and the Eighteenth Amendment to the

The 1915 sinking of the ocean liner *Lusitania*, which had been carrying American passengers, by a German U-boat helped harden many Americans' attitudes toward anything German, such as beer.

Constitution became law. Later that year, Congress passed the Volstead Act, establishing penalties for violators of the Eighteenth Amendment. On January 16, 1920, Prohibition took effect. Proponents of the new law called it the "Noble Experiment."

## THE ROARING TWENTIES

It did not take long for the government to realize that, constitutional amendment or not, people were still going to drink. Under the Volstead Act, people could keep all the beer, wine, and spirits they had obtained prior to July 1, 1919. In the six months prior to the effective date of the law, liquor worth some $500,000 was stolen out of government warehouses. A year after Prohibition became law, more than 31,000 people were arrested for violating the nation's liquor laws. That same year, federal agents said they had closed down more than 95,000 illegal stills. In 1925, agents reported busting some 175,000 illegal stills.

The Eighteenth Amendment shut down every saloon in America, but bars and taprooms were soon replaced by speakeasies—illegal saloons that sometimes operated quite openly, depending on the size of the bribes their owners paid politicians and police officers to ignore their operations. At the height of Prohibition, experts estimate, there were at least 200,000 speakeasies operating in the United States.

Gangsters soon took over the distribution and sale of illegal alcohol. In New York, mobsters "Dutch" Schultz and Charles "Lucky" Luciano established bootlegging as a highly-organized operation, giving birth to a criminal enterprise

Although alcohol was illegal during Prohibition, it proved impossible for law enforcement officials to completely stamp out the sale and consumption of alcohol. Here, two men, one holding a bottle of liquor, stand with their illegal "still," a piece of equipment used to distill alcohol, circa 1925.

that would branch out into narcotics, gambling, and prostitution. In Detroit, the bootlegging business was controlled by a group of thugs who called themselves the Purple Gang. They specialized in smuggling Canadian whiskey across the Michigan border. The Mayfield Road gang ran Cleveland. Philadelphia was under the thumb of a bootlegger named Waxey Gordon. But no bootlegging operation was as big, or as ruthless, as the Chicago mob under the leadership of the notorious Al Capone.

The extent of Capone's ruthlessness was displayed on St. Valentine's Day in 1929, when he dispatched a squad of killers to a Chicago garage that served as headquarters for a rival gang headed by George "Bugsy" Moran. When they arrived at the garage, Capone's hit men lined up Moran's gang against a wall and opened fire with machine guns. The St. Valentine's Day Massacre established Capone as the fearsome king of bootlegging in Chicago. It is believed that at the height of Capone's illegal empire, he earned between $60 million and $100 million a year on beer sales alone.

## ENFORCING THE LAW

The federal government struck back. In New York, Schultz spent years dodging indictments and was finally murdered by his own gang when they feared he was bringing down too much heat on them. Luciano was eventually sent to prison on a prostitution charge. And in Chicago, an elite squad of federal agents was established to break up Capone's bootlegging operation. The leader of the squad was a lawman from Cleveland named Eliot Ness. His agents became known as the "Untouchables" because they could not be bribed. Ness led raids on Capone's warehouses, distilleries, and breweries, bursting through the doors with weapons drawn. Ness would usually invite press photographers along for the ride, and made sure they got plenty of pictures as he took an axe to the barrels filled with Capone's beer. In his autobiography, *The Untouchables*, Ness described a typical raid:

> We started to knock them over with headline-catching regularity. . . . Using the same tactics, we closed down another big brewery at 3136 South Wabash Avenue a few days after the first successful raid. This one masqueraded as "The Old Reliable Trucking Company." We had one detail covering the roof, where two trap doors gave access to outside fire escapes; another battered in from the rear; and Basile, Gardner and I rode the truck in a smashing entrance through the front doors. . . . With every exit blocked . . . there was no escape for those inside and we netted five more prisoners. . . . We destroyed 40,324 gallons of unbarreled beer and 115 barrels which had already been racked. Then we loaded all the easily movable equipment on two more confiscated trucks that were now being added to our ever-growing fleet.

Despite the heroics of Eliot Ness and other gang-busters, efforts to enforce the Eighteenth Amendment met mostly with failure. Although hundreds of thousands of gallons of alcoholic beverages were seized in police raids, they represented a mere trickle when compared to the millions of gallons that were finding their way across the borders or smuggled in by boat onto remote beaches or manufactured in secret breweries and distilleries. In 1924, an estimated $40 million worth of liquor had been smuggled into the country. What's more, a provision of the Volstead Act permitted a small quantity of liquor to be made available for medical reasons. In 1928, it is estimated that American physicians earned $40 million writing prescriptions for whiskey. And the official statistics could not track the cheap "bathtub gin" that many Americans learned how to make in their own homes.

Government statistics showed that Prohibition was not stopping people from drinking. In 1914, according to federal studies, most American men started drinking

The headline of a Brooklyn newspaper from October 24, 1929, discusses the collapse of the stock market on what became known as "Black Thursday." The Stock Market Crash is often considered the starting point of the Great Depression.

at the age of 21. In 1923, after three years of Prohibition, the average starting age for male drinkers had dropped to 20. Also, more women were drinking during the 1920s, and they were starting at a younger age. In 1914, the average age at which American women started drinking was 28; by 1923, that age had been lowered to 25. Even top government officials flaunted the law. During the early 1920s, it was no secret around Washington, D.C., that President Warren G. Harding kept a well-stocked bar in the White House.

## REPEAL

During the 1928 presidential campaign, Democratic candidate Alfred E. Smith called for the repeal of Prohibition, while Republican candidate Herbert Hoover praised Prohibition as the "great social and economic experiment." Leaders of the Anti-Saloon League

supported Hoover, but their endorsement of the Republican probably had more to do with the fact that Smith was a Roman Catholic, and at the time few Americans were willing to elect a Catholic president. Observed the writer H.L. Mencken, "If [Al Smith] loses, it will be because those who fear the Pope outnumber those who are tired of the Anti-Saloon League." Hoover won by a wide margin, and took office in early 1929.

It can be argued that the death knell for Prohibition chimed on "Black Thursday"—October 24, 1929, the beginning of the U.S. stock market crash. Soon, the country would be plunged into the depths of a devastating depression, forcing millions of Americans out of work and into the soup lines. Before his arrest on prostitution charges, Lucky Luciano predicted that the troubles of the stock market would also mean troubles for the bootlegging business. According to *The Last Testament of Lucky Luciano*, the gangster told his friends, "The public won't buy it no more. When they ain't got nothin' else, they gotta have a drink or there's gonna be trouble. And they're gonna want to have that drink legal."

President Hoover bore the full political burden of the stock market crash and the Great Depression. In 1932, he lost in a landslide to Democrat Franklin D. Roosevelt, who had promised to repeal Prohibition during the campaign. Less than a month after Roosevelt took the oath of office, a bill proposing a constitutional amendment to repeal Prohibition was introduced in Congress. It sailed through the House and Senate and quickly won support from the state legislatures. On November 7, 1933, the final four state legislatures ratified the Twenty-First Amendment, providing the measure with the necessary 36 states needed for the amendment to become law.

Prohibition was repealed under the administration of President Franklin D. Roosevelt, who intended to fund his social programs with a tax on alcohol.

It should be pointed out that President Roosevelt had his own reasons for backing the repeal. With the country plagued by the Great Depression, Roosevelt proposed a number of social programs—known as the New Deal—aimed at rescuing people from poverty and restoring their hope. Roosevelt knew it would take hundreds of millions of dollars to pay for the New Deal. He intended to place a heavy federal tax on liquor sales and use the money to help fund his programs. Most people didn't mind the new tax—they just wanted a drink. After thirteen years, Prohibition was dead.

During the final months of Prohibition, few people observed the law and there was little enforcement of what had been one of America's most unpopular laws. And yet, for decades there remained a large number of people who still believed in the spirit of the law. In 1939, nearly 61 percent of respondents told a Gallup

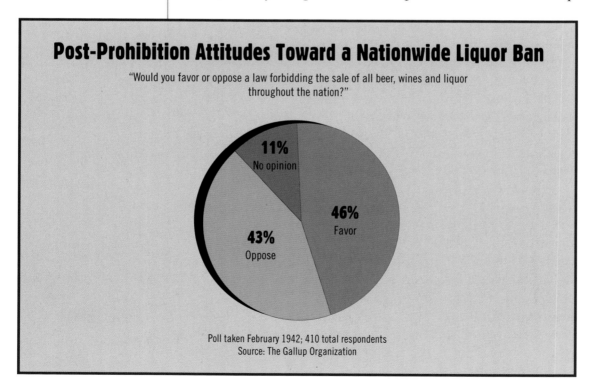

## Post-Prohibition Attitudes Toward a Nationwide Liquor Ban

"Would you favor or oppose a law forbidding the sale of all beer, wines and liquor throughout the nation?"

11%
No opinion

46%
Favor

43%
Oppose

Poll taken February 1942; 410 total respondents
Source: The Gallup Organization

poll that they never drink wine, beer, or liquor. In 1942, 46 percent of respondents to a Gallup poll said they continued to support a national law prohibiting the sales of alcohol while just 43 percent opposed the law, with 11 percent stating no opinion. In other words, a plurality of Americans endorsed the return of Prohibition. As the years passed, support for a national ban on alcohol sales would ebb, yet a significant minority of people would still find themselves believing that the consumption of beer, wine, and liquor is wrong. In 1958, nearly 29 percent of respondents to a Gallup poll said they continued to support a national law prohibiting the sale of alcoholic beverages.

## TELEVISION ADS PROMOTE ALCOHOL CONSUMPTION

After the end of World War II in 1945, servicemen returning from the military married their sweethearts, started families, bought homes, and started filling those homes with all manner of consumer products. Suddenly, millions of people were in the market for cars, refrigerators, air conditioners, and other appliances. At the top of nearly every shopping list, however, was the major innovation of the mid-20th century: a television set. In 1950, Gallup polls reported an average of 13 percent of households in America had a TV. Five years later, in 1955, Gallup polls reported an average of 73 percent of respondents had a television in their homes. And by 1959, Gallup found that nearly 90 percent of American homes included a TV set.

What were people watching? Certainly, comedy, and variety shows were popular; many of the first TV stars had also been popular on the radio, and they easily made the transition to the new medium. Quiz shows also made the transition to TV. Mysteries and dramas were also popular. During the 1950s, the television networks launched news programs, finding TV to be a highly successful medium for portraying the drama of everyday life. But when the networks discovered the popularity of televised sports, the medium truly took off. "Television got off the ground because of sports," former NBC sports director Harry Coyle said in an interview. "Today, maybe, sports needs television to survive, but it was just the opposite when it started. When we put on the World Series in 1947, heavyweight fights, the Army-Navy football game, the sales of television sets just spurted."

At first, beer companies were wary about advertising on television. After all, memories of Prohibition were still fresh in people's minds and brewers were afraid to offend potentially influential people. A 1939 Gallup poll reflected this sentiment, finding that 40 percent of respondents supported a bill in Congress that proposed to ban all forms of beer and liquor advertising. The bill eventually failed, but it was clear that many Americans were offended by public advertisements extolling the pleasures of drinking.

Nevertheless, it did not take long for beer companies to figure out that the customers they most wanted to reach—men with money in their pockets—were sports fans. In 1947, the year NBC first televised the World Series, few Americans owned television sets. The one place a baseball fan could be guaranteed to see the game was at the local tavern. During the series, fans endured standing-room-only crowds in taverns so they could watch the games on the tiny, black-and-white TV sets perched above the bars.

Soon, beer companies began to sponsor sports programming on television. Narragansett Beer sponsored the telecasts of Boston Red Sox games. In 1949, Jax Beer sponsored *Outdoors Louisiana*, a hunting and fishing show. Also that year, Griesedieck Beer sponsored a sports program on St. Louis TV hosted by Harry Caray, who went on to broadcast St. Louis Cardinals and Chicago Cubs games. Goebel Beer sponsored telecasts of Detroit Tigers games.

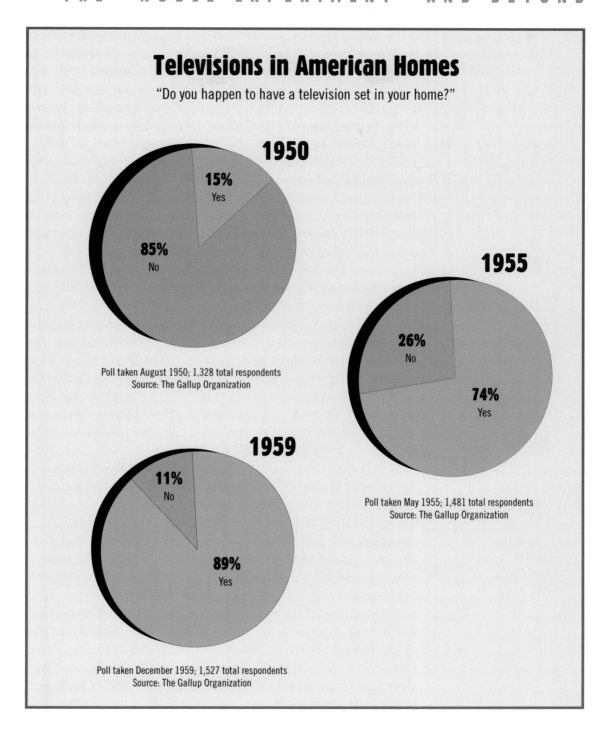

# Televisions in American Homes
"Do you happen to have a television set in your home?"

**1950**

15%
Yes

85%
No

Poll taken August 1950; 1,328 total respondents
Source: The Gallup Organization

**1955**

26%
No

74%
Yes

Poll taken May 1955; 1,481 total respondents
Source: The Gallup Organization

**1959**

11%
No

89%
Yes

Poll taken December 1959; 1,527 total respondents
Source: The Gallup Organization

Soon, beer commercials developed characters and themes to promote their product. In 1951, the Carling Brewing Company was the 28th largest brewery in the United States. That year, Carling hit the airwaves with ads featuring a barmaid named Mabel, who would appear carrying a tray of the company's Black Label beers after hearing a call for, "Hey Mabel! Black Label!" By 1957, thanks in part to Mabel's popularity, Carling had grown into the sixth-largest brewery in the United States. Other characters of the era included Bert and Harry Piel, the fictitious owners of the Piel Brothers brewery in Brooklyn, New York. The animated characters, voiced by the comedy team of Bob Elliott and Ray Goulding, became so popular that they had their own fan club with some 100,000 members.

Wine companies have long advertised on television and radio as well, but distillers of hard liquor did not start purchasing broadcast time until 1996. For decades, the manufacturers of spirits observed a voluntary ban on radio and TV advertising, but finally distillers decided they needed the electronic medium as well. "There's no basis for letting two forms of alcohol advertising, wine and beer, on television and radio and discriminating against another form," argued Fred A. Meister, president of the Distilled Spirits Council of the United States, a trade group representing liquor companies, in a 1996 *New York Times* article. Members of the Distilled Spirits Council decided to buy broadcast advertising time after one of the largest distillers in the world, Seagram Company, started running TV commercials on its own in selected markets.

Soon after the Seagram commercials started airing, a Gallup poll found that 63 percent of Americans opposed advertising "hard liquor" on television. Beer and wine commercials received relatively cool receptions as well; nearly 49 percent of respondents to the Gallup poll said they would like to see beer ads banned on television, while some 48 percent of respondents favored bans on wine commercials.

Despite this negative reaction to alcohol advertising, there is no question that commercials for alcohol dominate television broadcasting today—and not just in sports programming. According to the Center on Alcohol Marketing and Youth at Georgetown University, the alcohol industry spent $811 million on TV advertising in 2001, which paid for the airing of more than 200,000 commercials. Unfortunately, many of these advertisements appear during programs watched by young people—the Center on Alcohol Marketing and Youth organization found that 89 percent of those ads reached a youthful audience. This means that young people will continue to be inundated by advertisements that glorify alcohol use.

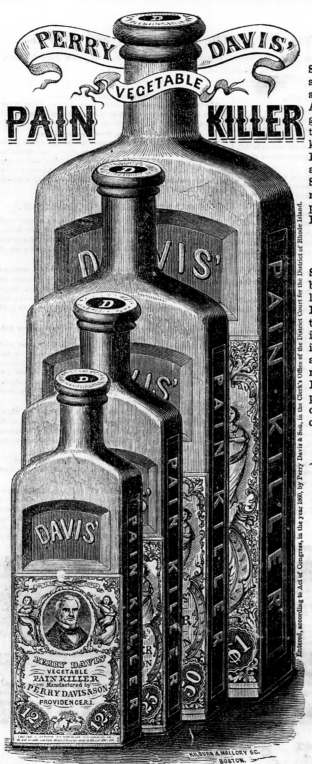

## PERRY DAVIS' VEGETABLE PAIN KILLER

### TAKEN INTERNALLY,
#### CURES

Sudden Colds, Coughs, Fever and Ague, Dyspepsia, Asthma and Phthisic, Liver Complaint, Acid Stomach, Headache, Indigestion, Heartburn, Canker in the Mouth and Stomach, Canker Rash, Kidney Complaints, Piles, Sea Sickness, Sick Headache, Cramp and Pain in the Stomach, Painters' Colic, Diarrhœa, Dysentery, Summer Complaint, Cholera Morbus, Cholera Infantum, and Cholera.

### APPLIED EXTERNALLY,
#### CURES

Scalds, Burns, Frost Bites, Chilblains, Sprains, Bruises, Whitlows, Felons, Boils, Old Sores, Ringworms, Rheumatic Affections, Headache, Neuralgia in in the Face, Toothache, Pain in the Side, Pain in the Back and Loins, Neuralgic or Rheumatic Pains in the Joints or Limbs, Stings of Insects, Scorpions, Centipedes, and the Bites of Poisonous Insects and Venomous Reptiles.

*A fresh supply of the*
**PAIN KILLER**
*just received and for sale by*

Entered, according to Act of Congress, in the year 1860, by Perry Davis & Son, in the Clerk's Office of the District Court for the District of Rhode Island.

KILBURN & MALLORY SC.
BOSTON.

# 3

# THE DRUG CULTURE

**M**ore than a century ago, a person with a headache may have tried to relieve the pain with a spoonful of McMunn's Elixir. Darby's Carminative could be used to treat diarrhea, while Ayer's Cherry Pectoral could help ease sore muscles. As for young children experiencing the pain of teething, a spoonful of Mrs. Winslow's Soothing Syrup would help quiet them down. Products like these were known as patent medicines, and by the 1890s there were hundreds available at the local pharmacy, through newspaper and magazine advertisements, or from door-to-door salesmen.

Prior to 1906, the one ingredient common to most patent medicines was opium, a powerful and addictive narcotic. The resin from the opium poppy can be distilled into morphine and heroin, two powerful, highly addictive, and dangerous drugs.

Today, the U.S. government spends hundreds of millions of dollars each year on programs to prevent cultivation of the opium poppy in Afghanistan, Thailand, and other distant countries, and billions more to stop the distribution of

So-called "patent medicines," like the painkiller pictured in the advertisement on the opposite page, often contained narcotic substances like opium.

heroin and other illegal drugs in the United States. But a century ago, Americans could purchase patent medicines laced with opium with relative ease, as long as they could afford the price of the bottle—typically a nickel or a dime.

And the makers of the patent medicines did not have to make a deal with an Asian drug lord to smuggle opium into the United States. In America, opium fields could be found in many places, particularly in the South, where opium was a cash crop. As opium's addictive and dangerous qualities became more widely known, some state legislatures banned cultivation of the plant, but many did not. Congress actually did not take action to pass a national law banning opium until 1942. According to *Licit and Illicit Drugs*, in 1871, S. Dana Hays, an official of the Massachusetts Board of Health, surveyed the availability of opium in his state and said:

> There are so many channels through which the drug may be brought into the State, that I suppose it would be impossible to determine how much foreign opium is used here; but it may easily be shown that the home production increases every year. Opium has been recently made from white poppies, cultivated for the purpose, in Vermont, New Hampshire, and Connecticut, the annual production being estimated by hundreds of pounds, and this has generally been absorbed in the communities where it is made. It has also been brought here from Florida and Louisiana, where comparatively large quantities are regularly sent east from California to Arizona, where its cultivation is becoming an important branch of industry, ten acres of poppies being said to yield, in Arizona, twelve hundred pounds of opium.

Opium was not the only drug finding its way into consumer products. In 1886, Georgia pharmacist John Styth Pemberton developed a syrup he called "Coca-Cola," which he advertised as effective in combating many ailments, including insomnia. Pemberton did not

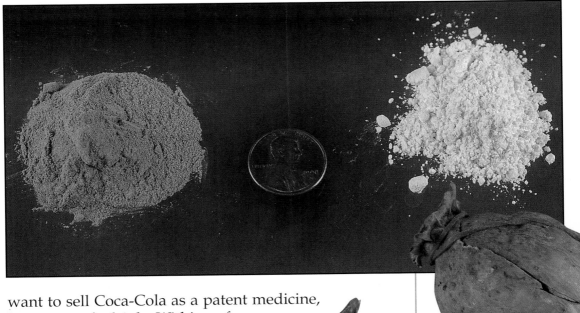

want to sell Coca-Cola as a patent medicine, but as a soft drink. Within a few years, Pemberton died and the formula for Coca-Cola passed into the hands of a new owner, pharmacist Asa Candler, who, according to *The Sparkling Story of Coca-Cola*, started advertising the product as a "delightful summer and winter beverage" that also "relieves mental and physical exhaustion" and could relieve headaches. Faithfully standing behind his product, Candler later revealed that he had decided to buy the formula for Coca-Cola because he suffered from severe and chronic headaches and indigestion; after sampling the drink he found that his bad feelings had gone away.

The fact is, Pemberton's formula for Coca-Cola included the extract of coca leaves, which the Inca Indians of South America had been chewing for centuries with a fervor because they found it gave them energy, cured their ills, and made them feel good. When the Spanish conquistadors arrived in South America during the 16th century and learned about the coca

The sap from the opium poppy (Papaver somniferum) can be distilled into the powerful drug heroin.

Coca-Cola was originally advertised as a refreshing beverage capable of curing headaches and insomnia. The drink's therapeutic benefits resulted from a small amount of cocaine in its original formula, which was eliminated in 1906.

plant, they found they could control the Incas and make them into slaves simply by withholding their coca leaves.

The very dangerous drug cocaine is also extracted from coca leaves, and in 1898, executives of the Coca-Cola company were forced to admit in court that their soft drink contained a very tiny amount of cocaine. A short time later, the company changed the formula to eliminate the drug, and the advertising was rewritten to emphasize the "delicious and refreshing" qualities of the drink, rather than its therapeutic value.

Another substance with a reputation as a "wonder drug" arrived in the United States at the end of the 19th century. Scientists at Bayer Pharmaceutical Company in Germany had developed the substance diacetylmorphine, which they extracted from the opium plant. Bayer called the new drug heroin, and claimed its product not only dulled pain but also helped people addicted to other drugs kick their habits. Starting in 1899, Bayer would sell a ton of heroin a year in the United States and other countries until the monstrous and addictive qualities of the drug became known, prompting federal authorities in 1924 to finally outlaw heroin.

As for the patent medicines, the U.S. Pure Food and Drug Act of 1906 spelled their eventual demise. The act required medicines containing opiates to list their ingredients on the labels. Later amendments to the act required the ingredients to meet standards of purity that the fly-by-night tonic and elixir makers could not possibly meet. In 1914, the Harrison Narcotics Act placed further controls on the availability of opiates and made it illegal to sell opiates to drug addicts. And during the 1920s, states started banning marijuana.

## A WIDESPREAD DRUG PROBLEM

The more restrictive laws did not prevent people from finding ways to get high. In 1918, Dr. A.G. Du Mez, secretary of the U.S. Public Health Service, issued a report outlining the extent of the drug addiction problem in the United States. Among his findings were that about a million Americans were regularly using opiates or cocaine, and that a widespread underground traffic in illegal drugs existed in the country. He claimed that "dope peddlers" imported the drugs across the Canadian and Mexican borders, and that despite the restrictions of the

Harrison Narcotics Act, in 20 U.S. cities the use of drugs had actually increased in the four years since the law was adopted.

By now, though, the people who were concerned about the widening threat of narcotics on American society had some difficulty convincing the government that the problem needed to be addressed. That is because the government was preoccupied with enforcing the nation's anti-drinking laws. The U.S. Treasury Department was responsible for enforcing the Volstead Act, as well as national laws regulating narcotics. However, the federal agents of the Treasury Department clearly regarded bootleggers, not drug dealers, as the nation's most dangerous criminals. Finally, in 1930 Congress created the Federal Bureau of Narcotics and placed at its helm Harry J. Anslinger, a former Prohibition agent.

## CELEBRITY DRUG USE

Prior to World War II, drugs were a little-noticed but nevertheless widespread problem in U.S. society. Following

## A MISGUIDED LOOK AT DRUG USE IN THE 1930s

In 1936, a church group sponsored the production of a film titled *Tell Your Children*, which told the story of two high school students, Bill and Mary, who discover marijuana at a party. In the film, the two innocent students and their friends become addicted to the drug; they suffer hallucinations and go insane. Finally, Mary is shot and killed.

*Tell Your Children* was cheaply made and featured no actors whom the public would recognize. Nevertheless, the film would enter American drug folklore. Ownership of the film eventually passed into the hands of filmmaker Dwain Esper, who reedited the movie, changed its title to *Reefer Madness*, and then made it available for a much wider distribution than it had received under its original title. Today, *Reefer Madness* is considered a cult classic. It is still screened regularly on college campuses and in art movie houses, where it is regarded as a humorous look at people's misconceptions about illegal drugs in the 1930s.

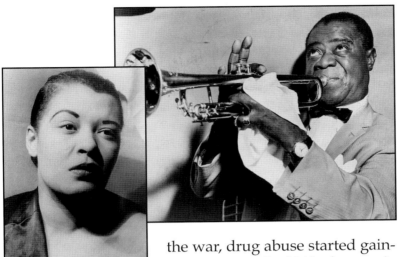

Over the years, many celebrities have become hooked on drugs. Among those addicted were the jazz singer Billie Holiday and musician Louis Armstrong.

the war, drug abuse started gaining attention. In 1949, the movie star Robert Mitchum was arrested at his girlfriend's home and charged with marijuana possession. Mitchum was convinced that his career would never recover from the scandal. "Well, this is the bitter end of everything—my career, my marriage, everything," he told his lawyer. Actually, both his marriage and his acting career survived. His wife forgave him, and after a 60-day sentence on a prison farm he was back in front of the cameras.

Other celebrities of the era also admitted to drug use. Movie stars Montgomery Clift and Bela Lugosi, musicians Chet Baker and John Coltrane, and singer Billie Holiday all suffered from addiction to narcotics. Author Jack Kerouac and other so-called Beat generation writers, who would have an enormous impact on the attitudes of rebellious young people during the 1950s and 1960s, wrote about their experiments with drugs. Saxophonist Charlie Parker, who revolutionized jazz by introducing the innovative free-form style known as bebop, became addicted to heroin as a teenager. When he died in 1955 at the age of 34, his body was so ravaged by drugs that the medical examiner initially estimated his age at between 50 and 60.

And Louis Armstrong, the trumpet player and singer who became one of the most beloved figures in American entertainment, smoked huge quantities of marijuana for much of his adult life. In a news interview, Laurence Bergreen, the author of the biography, *Louis Armstrong: An Extravagant Life*, talked about Armstrong's marijuana habit:

> This is one of the most difficult things about him to understand. He . . . often [said] that he was old enough to remember when booze was illegal and pot was legal because of course he came of age in the Prohibition era of the 1920s. And the idea was . . . that [marijuana] was healthy. Well, it was healthier than toxic moonshine, which was making other jazz musicians sick and even killing them. And he felt that it relaxed him a lot. So even though he got into trouble with the law a few years later for possession of marijuana, he continued to use it in very heavy quantities, you know, three cigar-sized joints a day, at least, throughout his life. Now, this did have a long-term harmful effect. I think if you talk to a doctor, they'll tell you that that amount of heavy, chronic marijuana use will have a bad effect on your lungs, for starters, and Louis did indeed suffer lung problems in his last—later years, and couldn't blow [trumpet] for a long period as a result.

There was definitely a drug problem in the United States. But relatively few Americans believed that drugs were invading their communities. In 1951, a Gallup poll asked Americans whether they thought teenagers in their communities were buying narcotics. Just 32 percent of the respondents said yes.

At the same time, though, many teenagers were finding out that they did not have to deal with a shady dope peddler to get high. In the early 1950s, toy companies started making scale-model kits available to hobbyists. The kits enabled children to assemble replicas of cars, airplanes, and ships. To build the models, glue that contained the solvent toluene had to be employed. A small tube of "airplane glue" produced for

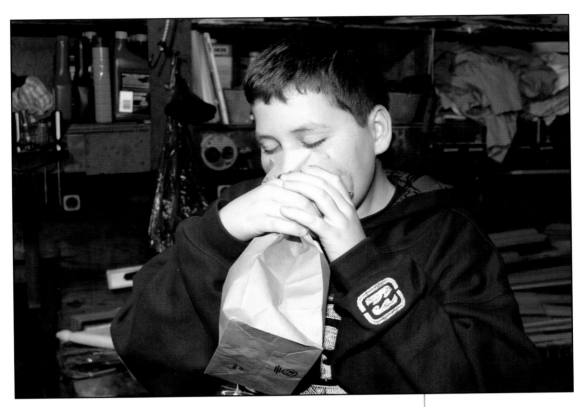

the young model maker was made available in every hobby store in the United States for a few cents. When inhaled directly from the tube, or sniffed out of a plastic bag or handkerchief, toluene can provide the user with a mind-numbing jolt. In 1961, a *New York Times* story reported, "Toxic fumes from a chemical ingredient in a model-airplane glue are being inhaled by some youngsters to obtain a feeling of elation similar to that of narcotics." Young people on Long Island, the newspaper reported, had discovered glue sniffing.

The practice of inhaling glue from a bag originated during the early 1960s. Inhaling the fumes of modeling glue and other substances can produce a "high" similar to that of illicit drugs.

## TURNING ON, TUNING IN, DROPPING OUT

The 1960s was a decade of rapid social change in the United States, particularly for young people. As opposition to the Vietnam War rose on college campuses, many students started questioning authority. They disagreed with the government about Vietnam and many times they disagreed with their parents on other issues as well. A youth-oriented drug culture emerged during the 1960s, the most famous symbol of which was the Haight-Ashbury neighborhood in San Francisco. By 1967, thousands of young people had flocked to Haight-Ashbury, where marijuana and other drugs were readily available. At San Francisco nightclubs such as the Matrix, rock bands like Jefferson Airplane, the Grateful Dead, and others performed songs heavily laced with drug themes.

By now, the so-called psychedelic drugs were also finding their way into the drug culture. The most widely abused of these was lysergic acid diethylamide (LSD). LSD, or "acid," was first discovered in 1943 by Swiss drug researchers. They found that LSD provided its user with a hallucinogenic high that included a kaleidoscopic variety of colorful sights and distracting

Colorfully decorated LSD "tabs" illustrate the psychedelic drug's hallucinogenic properties. The hours of wild visions provided by LSD made it extremely popular in the 1960s drug culture.

## Opinions of Timothy Leary

"From the highest position of plus 5 (someone you like very much) to the position of minus 5 (someone you dislike very much), how would you rate Timothy Leary?"

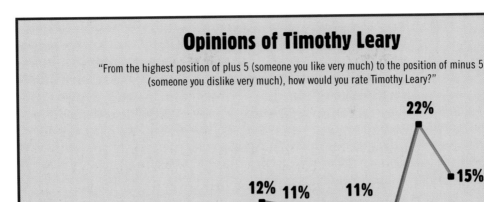

| +5 | +4 | +3 | +2 | +1 | -1 | -2 | -3 | -4 | -5 | Don't know |

3% 2% 4% 7% 12% 11% 7% 11% 7% 22% 15%

Poll taken November 1970; 1,061 college students
Source: The Gallup Organization

## Usage of LSD

"Have you ever tried LSD?"

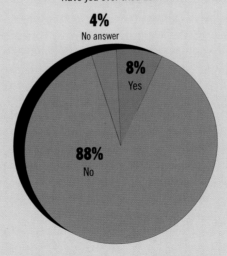

4%
No answer

8%
Yes

88%
No

Poll taken December 1969; 1,092 college students
Source: The Gallup Organization

sounds, usually lasting for several hours. LSD proved to be enormously popular in the drug culture, prompting the emergence of many self-proclaimed drug gurus who exhorted young people to experiment with acid. One of the most prominent of the drug gurus was Dr. Timothy Leary, a Harvard University psychology professor, who was first introduced to psychedelic drugs by the Beat poet Allen Ginsberg. By the end of the decade, Leary was encouraging young people to "turn on, tune in, and drop out." He was fired by Harvard and spent time in jail for promoting the use of illegal drugs, but some young people considered him a hero.

In 1969, a Gallup poll determined that 8 percent of college students had experimented with LSD. A year later, a Gallup poll asked college students to report their opinions about a number of people in the news, including Leary. Nearly 28 percent of the respondents said they held a positive opinion of Leary.

By the early 1970s, the drug culture had established a firm foothold in American society. Young people continued using drugs, despite the much-publicized drug-related deaths of some of the era's most prominent rock stars, among them Jimi Hendrix, Jim Morrison, and Janis Joplin. One of the best-selling books of the decade was *Fear and Loathing in Las Vegas* by counterculture journalist Hunter S. Thompson, who described his drug-addled trip to Nevada to cover a road race for *Sports Illustrated*. Early in the book, Thompson makes it clear that he intended to spend the entire trip to Las Vegas deep in the throes of a narcotic haze:

> The sporting editors had also given me $300 in cash, most of which was already spent on extremely dangerous drugs. The trunk of the car looked like a mobile police narcotics lab. We had two bags of grass, seventy-five pellets of mescaline, five sheets of high-powered blotter acid, a salt shaker half full of cocaine, and a whole galaxy of multi-colored uppers, downers,

screamers, laughers . . . and also a quart of tequila, a quart of rum, a case of Budweiser, a pint of raw ether and two dozen amyls . . . Not that we needed all that for the trip, but once you get locked into a serious drug collection, the tendency is to push it as far as you can.

## CHANGING ATTITUDES

By 1970, the U.S. Bureau of Narcotics reported that some 560,000 Americans were addicted to drugs—a tenfold increase over the number of drug addicts recorded in 1960. In response to the increasing problem of drug abuse, President Richard M. Nixon announced the most sweeping crackdown on drugs in American history. Speaking at a press conference in June 1971, Nixon called drug abuse "public enemy number one in the United States."

Nixon directed few resources toward rehabilitation of drug users or prevention programs for schools and other organizations involving young people. Instead, the president obtained $1 billion from Congress to fund a three-year federal attack on drugs. Part of Nixon's plan was establishment of Operation Intercept, which required U.S. Customs agents to search every car entering the United States from Mexico. As it turned out, Operation Intercept caught few drugs coming into the country, but it did cause intolerably long lines at the border crossings. A more significant accomplishment was the consolidation of several federal drug agencies into the U.S. Drug Enforcement Administration (DEA), which became the lead agency for all federal drug investigations.

Even though the DEA began targeting the underground drug culture, in the mid- to late-1970s a curious change occurred in the drug habits of Americans. Suddenly,

During the early 1970s, President Richard Nixon implemented a federal crackdown on illegal drugs. Singer Elvis Presley expressed support for this effort when he visited Nixon in December 1970. Ironically, Presley was addicted to painkillers, which may have contributed to his death in 1977.

drug abuse became chic, and movie stars, rock stars, supermodels and other celebrities were quite open about their drug use. An epicenter of the celebrity drug culture was Studio 54, a hip disco in New York City that opened in 1977. Anybody wondering what was going on inside just needed to glance at the neon sign hanging on the wall outside the club. It pictured the man in the moon inhaling cocaine from a spoon. Outside, tabloid photographers snapped pictures of Elizabeth Taylor, Liza Minelli, Andy Warhol, Mick and Bianca Jagger, the fashion designer Halston, and other celebrities as they floated in and out of the club. Inside the club, lines of cocaine were snorted freely.

In 1977, *Newsweek* magazine reported, "among hostesses in the smart sets of Los Angeles and New York, a little cocaine, like Dom Perignon [champagne] and Beluga caviar, is now de rigueur at dinners. Some partygoers pass it around along with the canapés on silver trays . . . the user experiences a feeling of potency, of confidence, of energy."

Of course, there was a dark story behind the cocaine that found its way into the glittering Manhattan disco scene. Some 3,000 miles south of New York, ruthless drug kingpins had turned the South American nation of Colombia into a virtual drug paradise. Colombian drug cartels centered in Medellín, Calí, and other Colombian cities developed cocaine empires, supervising the product from its cultivation in remote jungles to the refinement, packaging, shipment, and delivery of the drug to street dealers in the United States. Drug kingpins such as Jose Gonzalo Rodriguez, Pablo Escobar, and the Ochoa brothers made billions of dollars, controlled politicians, financed private security forces, and, essentially established their own laws. The extent of their ruthlessness became evident when, in 1975, Colombian police seized 600 kilograms of cocaine from a small airplane at an airport in Calí. In response, the Medellín drug

kingpins ordered the murders of 40 people responsible for letting the drugs fall into the hands of the police. Throughout the 1970s, most Americans remained unaware of the threat posed by the Colombian drug cartels. That situation began changing in 1982 when U.S. drug agents seized more than 3,900 pounds of cocaine—valued at some $100 million—from a hangar at Miami International Airport.

A new cocaine-related threat began emerging in the early 1980s. Street dealers learned how to cook cocaine into a cheap but potent form of the drug known as crack. Smoking crack gave the user a quicker and harder jolt than powdered cocaine and was also more addictive. As a result, crack addiction soon swept through American neighborhoods.

Powdered cocaine emerged as a glamorous status symbol during the 1970s.

During the late 1980s, a dangerous form of cocaine, known as crack, became available in American cities. Crack is cheaper, more potent, and more addictive than powdered cocaine. (Top) Dealers get crack in larger pieces and break them up for street sales. (Bottom) A street dose, broken up for consumption.

## NEW DRUG THREATS

The Colombian drug cartels eventually became far less influential, thanks to a crackdown by Colombian police prompted by international pressure and infighting among the cartels themselves. The U.S. government also contributed to disrupting the cocaine trade. By the 1990s many leaders of the Colombian cartels had either been killed in shootouts with police, jailed by the Colombian courts, or murdered by their own gangs. In 2000, President Bill Clinton authorized "Plan Colombia," making $1.3 billion available annually to the Colombian military to purchase helicopters and other equipment used to stop drug smugglers, to train soldiers and drug agents, and to reimburse farmers for not growing coca leaves. Although Plan Colombia has not wiped out the Colombian drug trade, drug trafficking in that country is no longer carried out with the assent of police and politicians.

The federal government also took steps to crack down on street dealers in the United States. In 1986, Congress passed the Anti-Drug Abuse Act, establishing mandatory minimum sentences for people caught selling drugs. Congress was prompted to act largely because of the death of Len Bias, a college basketball star who celebrated his selection in the National Basketball Association (NBA) draft by overdosing on cocaine. In July 1986, shortly after Bias's death, a Gallup poll asked Americans to rate the abused substances they believed posed the most dangers in society. Alcohol finished first on the list with 34 percent, but crack cocaine finished second at 22 percent and other

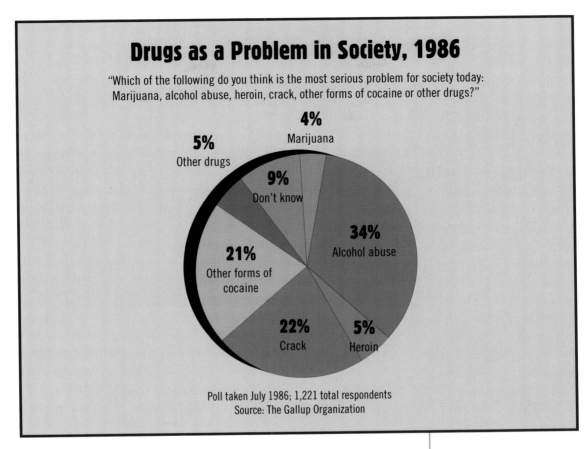

## Drugs as a Problem in Society, 1986

"Which of the following do you think is the most serious problem for society today: Marijuana, alcohol abuse, heroin, crack, other forms of cocaine or other drugs?"

4%
Marijuana

5%
Other drugs

9%
Don't know

34%
Alcohol abuse

21%
Other forms of cocaine

22%
Crack

5%
Heroin

Poll taken July 1986; 1,221 total respondents
Source: The Gallup Organization

forms of cocaine finished third at 21 percent. It is evident that Bias's death, as well as the ongoing crack epidemic in the United States, had awakened people to the threats posed by drugs.

By the start of the 21st century, new drugs had surfaced to threaten American society. One drug of particular concern was a new form of methamphetamine, known as crystal meth, ice, or crank. Crystal meth is a far more potent form of the methamphetamine (known as speed) that was swallowed on the streets of Haight-Ashbury a generation ago. Crystal meth labs have invaded many towns; amateur "cooks" can whip up a batch of the highly addictive drug with chemicals available in most hardware stores. In 2005, a Gallup poll

Crystal methamphetamine is a very dangerous drug. It is becoming more common, particularly in rural America.

asked respondents to name their top crime fears. Sixty-six percent of the respondents said the sexual abuse of children was their main concern, but the use or sale of crystal meth came in a close second at 65 percent.

## CHANGING ATTITUDES TOWARD DRUG USE

Twenty years after the famous Woodstock Rock Festival, the Gallup Organization wanted to know whether members of the generation that so readily accepted drugs in 1969 still believed in turning on, tuning in, and dropping out. In the 1989 poll, 42 percent of respondents between 30 and 49 years old said that during the 1960s and 1970s, they had smoked marijuana. Fifteen percent said they had experimented with LSD or harder drugs. Asked whether the era's liberal attitude toward marijuana and other drugs was good or bad, 83 percent of the respondents said bad.

A Gallup analysis concluded, "Interviews with the public at large—as well as with some who attended the event itself—suggest that, in a society beset by

# THE PRESIDENTS AND SUBSTANCE ABUSE

Two American presidents have admitted to substance abuse as young men, but neither Bill Clinton nor George W. Bush suffered political fallout when drinking and drug abuse incidents in their backgrounds came to light.

As Clinton campaigned for the presidency in 1992, newspapers reported that as a student at Oxford University in England in 1968, Clinton had smoked marijuana at a party. Eventually, Clinton confessed that it was true—although he claimed that when the marijuana cigarette was passed his way, he didn't breathe in the smoke. He said, "I've never broken a state law, but when I was in England I experimented with marijuana a time or two, and I didn't like it. I didn't inhale and never tried it again."

Clinton's political opponents aired television commercials that year publicizing the candidate's experimentation with marijuana. A Gallup poll showed that the commercials prompted 24 percent of voters to have a less favorable opinion of Clinton, while 9 percent said they found the candidate to be more favorable due to the commercials. However, most voters said the marijuana charge had not influenced their opinion of the candidate: the Gallup poll reported that 65 percent of voters said the TV commercials had not affected their view of Clinton. That fall, Clinton won the first of his two terms as president.

In 2000, as George W. Bush campaigned for the presidency, he was forced to admit that he had been arrested for driving under the influence of alcohol in 1976, while he was visiting his family's summer home in Kennebunkport, Maine. A police officer had noticed Bush driving erratically and pulled him over. At the Kennebunkport police station, a test showed Bush's blood-alcohol level was over the legal limit. He pleaded guilty, paid a $150 fine, and lost his driver's license for a month—typical penalties for drunken driving in the 1970s.

Again, voters were willing to look past the incident. A Gallup poll taken shortly before the November 2000 election reported that 87 percent of voters said Bush's arrest would not make them more likely or less likely to vote for him. Bush went on to win the election, and was reelected in 2004.

AIDS and crack cocaine, the drug culture and sexual promiscuity of Woodstock seem not only excessive, but downright dangerous. A 36-year-old California housewife who now has three children and works for a phone company recalls Woodstock: 'The music was great, there was a sense of togetherness, but the drugs got in the way . . . But I didn't feel that way then.'"

# 4 DRIVING UNDER THE INFLUENCE

Studies have shown that drivers who have been drinking alcohol or using drugs have slower reaction times and do not make good decisions when behind the wheel.

People who drink or use drugs before driving are a varied lot: men and women, young and old, wealthy and poor, "recreational" users and hard-core addicts. All of these people share one characteristic, however—invariably, most of them will get into trouble if they drive while under the influence of alcohol or drugs.

Sometimes, people who drink and drive are famous. In 2003, country and western singer Glen Campbell was arrested near his home in Phoenix, Arizona, and charged with driving under the influence. He pleaded guilty to "extreme drunken driving" and leaving the scene of an accident, and was sentenced to ten nights in jail and two years on probation.

Another celebrity who faced drunken driving charges was publicly contrite. After Olympic swimming star Michael Phelps was arrested for drunken driving near his Maryland home in 2004, the winner of six gold medals at the 2004 Olympic Games told a *Baltimore Sun* reporter, "I made a mistake. Getting into a car with anything to drink is wrong, dangerous and unacceptable. I'm nineteen, but no matter how old you are, you should take responsibility for your actions, which I will do. I'm extremely sorry for the mistake that I made."

At 19, Phelps was two years younger than the minimum drinking age in Maryland. The swimmer pleaded guilty, was placed on probation for 18 months, and as part of his court-ordered community service was required to make speeches to high school students about the dangers of drinking and driving.

Other celebrities who have faced driving under the influence (DUI) charges in recent years included Nick Carter of the singing group Backstreet Boys and actor Chris Klein, who starred in the film *American Pie* and its sequel. In Klein's case, the actor was arrested in Encinitas, California, with a blood alcohol level of 0.20, more than twice California's legal limit of 0.08.

Sometimes, people who drink and drive are people who should know better. In 2004, Peg Lautenschlager, the attorney general of Wisconsin, was arrested on DUI charges after she drove a state-owned car into a ditch near Madison, Wisconsin. Lautenschlager's blood alcohol level was 0.12, which is higher than the state's legal limit of 0.08. She insisted that she had consumed only two glasses of wine before the accident. Still, she received a citation for the offense.

"Tuesday was a difficult day for me of reflection," the attorney general said shortly after her arrest. "As a mom, a daughter, and a wife, I had to tell my family what I had done and what they would read, and hear, and see about me in the coming days. And Tuesday was a difficult day for me because I needed to tell my colleagues at the Wisconsin Department of Justice, an institution for which I have the utmost respect, that the boss had let them down."

Drinking and driving is more common at certain times of the year, such as holidays. In May 2005, police in East Baton Rouge, Louisiana, reported that they had arrested 11 people for drunken driving during Memorial Day weekend. The offenders ranged in age from 19 to 76. Four of the drivers were arrested while operating their cars with expired or suspended licenses. One of the arrestees was carrying an open container of alcohol in the car when he was pulled over. Another arrestee got into an accident and left the scene, and when the police caught up with him he scuffled with the arresting officer, finally striking the policeman. Everybody who was arrested that weekend went to jail.

Oddly enough, sometimes people who drink and drive do not drive cars. In 2005, police arrested Adam Reibolt, a 25-year-old Deshler, Ohio, man, on suspicion of drunken driving after he drove his lawn tractor into a ditch at two o'clock in the morning. Police said Reibolt told them he had been drinking beer before deciding to mow the lawn. He was charged with drunken driving after police said he failed a field sobriety test.

Of a far more serious nature was the charge leveled against John V. Salamone of North Coventry, Pennsylvania. In 2004, Salamone was convicted of piloting a small airplane while drunk. He was sentenced to a prison term of six to 23 months and ordered to relinquish ownership of his $34,000 airplane.

Without question, the most serious ramification of mixing alcohol and motor vehicles is that people who drink and drive can kill people. Between 1995 and 2004, according to the advocacy group Mothers Against Drunk Driving (MADD), 171,408 people lost their lives in drunken driving accidents on American roads. That averages out to roughly 47 people a day killed by drunk drivers, every single day, for the past 10 years.

## TOO DRUNK TO DRIVE

Alcohol slows a person's reaction time. It dulls the reflexes and impairs judgment, making it hard for the driver to pay attention to what he or she is doing. At the same time, alcohol often gives drivers a false sense of security; many drunk drivers do not realize they are in no condition to drive.

The first law banning drinking and driving was passed in 1910—when there were few cars on the roads—by the state of New York. California passed its drunken driving law a year later. Since then all states have enacted statutes making it a crime to drive while intoxicated, either by alcohol or drugs.

For decades, most states treated driving under the influence as a relatively minor offense. During the

The president of Mothers Against Drunk Driving (MADD), an influential advocacy organization, addresses a crowd. Groups like MADD have successfully lobbied many states to lower the legal blood-alcohol limit for drivers.

1970s and 1980s, however, MADD and other advocacy groups pressured state and federal legislators to increase the penalties for DUI. The lawmakers responded by establishing heavy fines and jail terms for people arrested for driving while under the influence. State legislatures, and subsequently Congress, also raised the legal drinking age to 21.

This was not the first time the drinking age had been set at that level. Following the repeal of Prohibition in 1933, most states had established 21 as the minimum legal drinking age, or MLDA. During the 1960s, though, Congress enacted a draft of men as young as 18 to supply troops to the Vietnam War. When the young men returned from duty overseas, they had two complaints: they were not old enough to vote or to drink legally. For a government that considered them old enough to die for their country, there were no easy answers to those questions. So Congress lowered the voting age to 18, and many of the states—which regulate alcohol sales—lowered the legal drinking age.

Soon, however, the effects of the lower drinking age were evident, particularly on the highways. Drunken driving by young people became a major national concern. Studies found that most young people did not drink responsibly, and in 1976 states started raising their MLDAs.

In 1984, Congress passed the Uniform Drinking Age Act, which mandated that federal highway funds would be withheld from any state that did not raise its MLDA to 21. Because states rely heavily on the federal government to supply money for road construction and repair, the states that still had a MLDA below 21 raised their minimum drinking ages, although some states succeeded in delaying the implementation of the law for many years. In Louisiana, where the economy of New Orleans depends largely on the party atmosphere of the French Quarter, officials managed to delay implementation of the MLDA of 21 until 1995. Finally, though, Louisiana officials gave in to federal pressure. Today, it is illegal for anyone in the United States who is not at least 21 years old to buy alcoholic beverages.

To determine whether a driver is intoxicated, law-enforcement officials test for the alcohol content of the driver's blood. This can be determined by a test of a blood sample, which is often drawn in a hospital emergency room, or in a test conducted on the streets by the so-called "breathalyzer," a machine employed by police that requires the driver to blow into a tube. The machine then analyzes the alcohol content of the driver's saliva. By 2002, all but seventeen states had adopted the standard of 0.08 as legally intoxicated. It means that if the alcohol content of a

A police officer administers a "breathalyzer" test to a motorist, to determine how much the driver has had to drink.

person's blood or saliva is 8/100 of 1 percent, he or she is considered drunk and should not be operating a vehicle.

In the seventeen other states, the standards of 0.10 or 0.12 were observed. However, those states started lowering their blood alcohol thresholds as well, following adoption of a federal law that gave them four years to establish tougher standards or risk losing federal highway improvement funds.

Over the years, most Americans have favored tough laws regulating drinking and driving. Even as far back as 1967, a Gallup poll found Americans supporting harsh measures. Back then, jail terms for drunk drivers were rare, but a Gallup poll taken in 1967 found 44 percent of respondents favoring jail time for people who consumed more than one drink and then got behind the wheel of a car. In 2000, after states got tough with drunk drivers, a Gallup poll sponsored by MADD and General Motors found that 72 percent of respondents favored the tougher blood alcohol threshold of 0.08.

## DRUG USE AND DRIVING

Driving under the influence is not limited to consumption of alcoholic beverages. People who abuse drugs can also be impaired when they drive. This fact is sadly borne out by the tragic stories that regularly appear in the media of drug-addled drivers taking the lives of innocent victims, such as the following examples:

✓ In 2004, 19-year-old Michael Joseph Whitton of Utah was sentenced to 30 years in prison after pleading guilty to killing two children and critically injuring a third who were struck by his car while playing in their front yard. Whitton admitted to using marijuana and methamphetamine before getting into his car.

✓ In 2003, Patrick Presley, a 31-year-old Mississippi man, was convicted on charges of driving under the influence and causing the death of a 37-year-old woman. A distant relative of the late rock 'n' roll star Elvis Presley, Patrick was found to have used methamphetamine before the accident. He died in his prison cell while awaiting sentencing, a victim of suicide.

✓ In 1999, five high school students died when their car hit a tree in Lima, Pennsylvania. The local medical examiner said the driver of the car, a 16-year-old girl, had been huffing an inhalant shortly before the crash. Three other girls in the car had also been huffing, tests showed.

In 2000, the U.S. National Highway Traffic Safety Administration (NHTSA) enlisted a panel of toxicologists—scientists who study the affect of chemicals and other substances on the human body and human performance—and charged them with the task of assessing the effects of drugs on the performance of drivers. The toxicologists studied 16 drugs and similar substances, including some that are legally available as over-the-counter medications as well as drugs available only through prescriptions. In addition, several illegal drugs—including cocaine, marijuana, methamphetamine, and LSD—were studied. The toxicologists conducted the study to determine whether people under the influence of those drugs could safely operate motor vehicles. In all the drugs that were studied, the toxicologists found reason to believe that the substances impair the ability of drivers to negotiate the roads.

For example, the toxicologists determined that a hit of crack could provide a narcotic effect within as little as 30 seconds, and that the user would likely feel the effects for one or two hours. Purer forms of cocaine also act quickly, the toxicologists said. As for how

Illegal drugs, prescription drugs, alcohol, and inhalants can all impair a person's ability to drive safely.

cocaine users operate their cars, the NHTSA study stated, "Observed signs of impairment in driving performance have included subjects speeding, losing control of their vehicle, causing collisions, turning in front of other vehicles, high-risk behavior, inattentive driving, and poor impulse control. As the effects of cocaine wear off subjects may suffer from fatigue, depression, sleepiness, and inattention. Cocaine may enhance performance of simple tasks but not complex, divided-attention tasks such as driving."

As for marijuana, the NHTSA study said:

> The short term effects of marijuana use include problems with memory and learning, distorted perception, difficulty in thinking and problem-solving, and loss of coordination. Heavy users may have increased difficulty sustaining attention, shifting attention to meet the demands and changes in the environment, and in registering, processing and using information. . . . The ability to concentrate and maintain attention are decreased during marijuana use, and impairment of hand-eye coordination is dose-related over a wide range of dosages. . . . Low doses of [marijuana] moderately

impair cognitive and psychomotor tasks associated with driving, while severe driving impairment is observed with high doses, chronic use and in combination with low doses of alcohol. The more difficult and unpredictable the task, the more likely marijuana will impair performance.

Methamphetamine users were also found to be impaired. The NHTSA report said typical behaviors by meth-abusing drivers include "speeding, lane travel, erratic driving, accidents, nervousness, rapid and non-stop speech, unintelligible speech, disorientation, agitation, staggering and awkward movements, irrational and violent behavior, and unconsciousness."

Methamphetamine is a derivative of the amphetamines that were developed in the 1920s and originally used to treat people suffering from asthma. Soon, it was found that amphetamines also had stimulating qualities—they could wake people up and make them more active. In 2000, a troubling study released by the U.S. Substance Abuse and Mental Health Services Administration (SAMHSA) reported that many long-haul truck drivers abuse methamphetamines in order to stay awake longer and, therefore, drive their trucks longer distances. Said the report:

> Because of the sense of increased energy that methamphetamine supplies to users, it is often used in the workplace. Use by a truck driver who drives long distances for long hours on America's highways jeopardizes the safety of both the driver who uses and those who share the road. In a sample of fatally injured drivers, methamphetamine use was found to be 7.3 percent. Some researchers say that these findings seem to "support a casual relationship between methamphetamine use and an increased risk of fatal accident involvement.

The SAMHSA report was based on interviews with twenty truck drivers who were approached at truck stops along Interstate 10 in Arizona during March 1998. "Three of the twenty truck drivers interviewed had used methamphetamine," said the study. "An

Some truck drivers abuse methamphetamines in order to stay awake at the wheel, impairing their ability to drive and even causing serious accidents.

additional nine said they knew another truck driver who used methamphetamine well enough to answer some of the questions about use. Of twenty drivers, eighteen had used some form of stimulant to stay alert on the road. The stimulants used included coffee, caffeine pills, and amphetamines as well as cocaine and methamphetamine. . . . Of the twenty drivers, seventeen said that methamphetamine is easy to get. They reported that it is available in the back lots of most truck stops, easily obtained via citizens band radio contacts, and sold by both drivers and local dealers."

## A NATIONAL CRISIS

Driving under the influence of alcohol or drugs has grown into a national crisis. Despite tough laws and negative public attitudes toward driving under the influence, Americans still drink or use drugs and drive in large numbers.

It is evident that the message about the dangers of driving while impaired has not gotten through to enough people. According to MADD, 1.5 million drivers were arrested in 2002 on charges of driving under the influence. That number represents one driver for every 130 licensed drivers in the United States. And many of those people were repeat offenders—according to MADD's statistics, 1,461 fatal accidents that occurred in 2001 involved drivers that already had at least one DUI conviction on their records.

And there is no question that many drunk drivers are under the age of 21. According to a 2005 Gallup poll,

# Teens and Drinking

"Do you have occasion to use alcoholic beverages such as liquor, wine, or beer?"
(Percentage of U.S. teens aged 13-17 saying "yes")

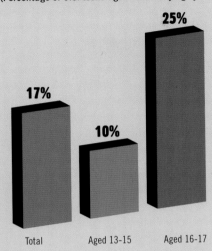

17%

10%

25%

Total          Aged 13-15          Aged 16-17

"Have you ever been a passenger in a car when a driver about your own age was under the influence of alcohol?"
(Percentage of U.S. teens aged 13-17 saying "yes")

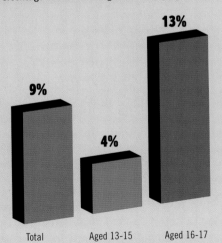

9%

4%

13%

Total          Aged 13-15          Aged 16-17

Gallup Youth Surveys taken January-February 2005; 1,028 total respondents
Source: The Gallup Organization

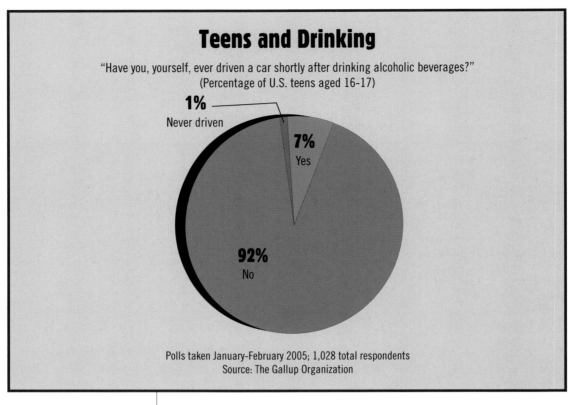

## Teens and Drinking

"Have you, yourself, ever driven a car shortly after drinking alcoholic beverages?"
(Percentage of U.S. teens aged 16-17)

**1%**
Never driven

**7%**
Yes

**92%**
No

Polls taken January-February 2005; 1,028 total respondents
Source: The Gallup Organization

17 percent of young people between the ages of 13 and 17 admit they have consumed alcoholic beverages. Among respondents aged 16 and 17—the ages at which most teens get their drivers' licenses—25 percent admit they have used alcohol. Not surprisingly, some of those teens admitted to drinking and driving. Said a Gallup analysis:

> Teens can be dangerous drivers, either from a lack of maturing or experience—and adding alcohol to the equation is lethal. According to the National Highway Traffic Safety Administration, the percentage of non-alcohol-related fatalities involving teen drivers was 74.7 percent in 2003, and the percentage of alcohol-related fatalities involving teen drivers was 25.3 percent.

> Data from the Gallup Youth Survey suggest that a non-trivial number of teens have experienced impaired

driving firsthand. Nine percent of teens report having been a passenger in a car driven by someone about their age who was under the influence of alcohol. Not surprisingly, this percentage increases among teens of legal driving age. Four percent of thirteen- to fifteen-year-olds say they have ridden with a teen driver under the influence, compared with 13 percent of sixteen- and seventeen-year-olds.

A small but not insignificant number of teens report having driven a car shortly after drinking alcohol. Seven percent of sixteen- and seventeen-year-olds say they have. Obviously, thirteen- to fifteen-year-olds aren't of legal driving age and therefore don't report driving after drinking . . . Social desirability and legal factors could affect the way teens respond to this question, so the actual percentage of teens who have driven after drinking could be higher.

# HALL OF JUSTICE
\* \* \* \*

TO THE FAITHFUL AND
IMPARTIAL ENFORCEMENT
OF THE LAWS·WITH EQUAL
AND EXACT JUSTICE TO
ALL·OF WHATEVER STATE
OR PERSUASION·THIS
BUILDING IS DEDICATED
BY THE PEOPLE OF THE
CITY AND COUNTY OF
SAN FRANCISCO

ERECTED

AIDS PATIENT
NOT A CRIMINAL

Medical Cannabis Patient: Bruce Blackman, A
SafeAccessNow.

**PRESIDENT BUSH,**

**STOP
ARRESTING
MEDICAL
MARIJUANA
PATIENTS**

**www.SafeAccessNow.org**

BUSH
GUILTY
OF
TARGETTING
STATES'
RIGHTS

# LIBERALIZING AMERICA'S LAWS

**A** tourist who visits Amsterdam in the Netherlands can walk into any one of the city's many coffeehouses and light up a marijuana cigarette. Officially, smoking pot is illegal in the Netherlands, but Dutch authorities do not prosecute people who possess small quantities of marijuana or hashish for personal use. Smoking the drug is illegal on the streets, but in the city's coffeehouses and bistros, enjoying marijuana is an accepted part of Amsterdam nightlife.

In most other European countries, smoking marijuana remains a crime, but recent laws have taken much of the sting out of getting caught. In Spain, using marijuana is punishable by fine only. In Luxembourg, authorities have removed marijuana possession from the criminal code and have made it a civil offense, punishable by a small fine. In Italy, a first offense typically earns the marijuana user a warning; repeat offenders are encouraged to visit social workers. In Belgium, where marijuana had been outlawed since 1921, the government decriminalized the drug in 2001, permitting anybody to

(Opposite) Medicinal marijuana patients stage a demonstration in San Francisco, July 2005. Although marijuana effectively eases the pain of certain chronic illnesses, in 2005 the U.S. Supreme Court ruled that the federal government may prosecute those who grow, prescribe, or use the drug.

possess small amounts for personal use. In Germany, possession of a small amount of marijuana is regarded as a crime, but courts have ruled people should not be prosecuted for the offense. And in Britain and France, police have been instructed not to arrest people for possessing small quantities of marijuana.

Peter Pennekamp, director of the Dutch Health Ministry, told a reporter that governments across Europe have decided that people who enjoy smoking marijuana cigarettes from time to time should not be considered criminals. Certainly, he said, European governments do not encourage drug use, but they have come to realize that people who use drugs should be given positive reasons for giving up drugs, not confronted with criminal penalties if they are caught. "The fundamental point is that this is a public-health problem more than a law-and-order problem," said Pennekamp.

Americans who are hoping for a similar shift in attitude by their government are likely in for a long wait. Few federal, state, or local government leaders are interested in decriminalizing marijuana or any other drug. Police agencies concentrate on nailing the big-time drug kingpins as well as the street dealers, but arrests of otherwise law-abiding Americans in possession of small amounts of marijuana are also common. In fact, according to the advocacy group National Organization for Reform of Marijuana Laws (NORML), a pot smoker is arrested somewhere in the United States every 42 seconds.

## LIBERALIZED LAWS

Some states have liberalized their laws regarding marijuana. For example, eight states—California, Colorado, Maine, Minnesota, Mississippi, Nebraska, Nevada, and Ohio—have made possession of one ounce or less of marijuana a crime that is not punishable by jail time. Nevertheless, laws restricting drug possession and use remain on the books in all 50 states. And in some states, the penalties for simple possession can still be quite harsh. In 20 states, people convicted of possession of marijuana can be sent to jail for as long as a year. Tennessee's maximum penalty for marijuana possession is six years in prison, while Florida's maximum penalty is five years.

Most of those laws are aimed at people who cultivate crops of marijuana and who would be in possession of large quantities. Yet some of the laws still affect the recreational user. A pot smoker caught with 1.5 ounces of marijuana in Tennessee can face the state's harshest sentence.

NORML has long lobbied for a liberalization of laws governing pot. The organization notes that 755,187 Americans were arrested for marijuana possession in 2003. "These numbers belie the myth that police do not target and arrest minor marijuana offenders," said NORML Executive Director Keith Stroup in a 2004 press release. "This effort is a tremendous waste of criminal justice resources, costing American taxpayers $7.6 billion dollars annually. These dollars would be better served combating serious and violent crime, including the war on terrorism."

Stroup insisted that most of the arrestees obtained their pot for personal use. He pointed out that of the 755,187 people taken into custody on possession charges in 2003, only 92,301 were also charged with selling marijuana. That means the vast majority of arrestees— 662,886 people—were arrested for recreational use of marijuana. He said, "Arresting adults who smoke marijuana responsibly needlessly destroys the lives of thousands of otherwise law abiding citizens each year."

Possessing even a small amount of marijuana can lead to a hefty fine and, in many states, a jail sentence. The harshest marijuana laws chiefly target those who cultivate large quantities of the drug.

Across the United States, protests surface from time to time, led by activists who call for legalization of marijuana. Most demonstrations occur on college campuses. Many demonstrations are staged each year on April 20, which has turned into an unofficial national holiday for legalization activists. (Evidently, this tradition was launched in 1971 by a group of California students who met at 4:20 P.M. each day to get high. The term "420" became an unofficial code for pot smokers, who eventually adopted April 20, or 4/20, as the day they make their annual call for legalization. Most of the April 20 rallies are staged at 4:20 P.M.)

## THE DEBATE OVER LEGAL MARIJUANA

Unlike the students at 420 rallies, most government leaders are hardly enthusiastic about decriminalizing marijuana. One public official who did go on the record was Gary Johnson, a former governor of New Mexico who —

Two young women share a marijuana joint at a rally in Washington, D.C., to promote the legalization of pot. April 20 is the traditional date for such protests.

while in office—advocated legalization of marijuana as well as harder drugs, including cocaine and heroin.

Johnson insisted that the war on drugs had been a multibillion-dollar failure. Instead of continuing the war, Johnson advocated placing drug distribution under government control. By legalizing drugs, he said, the government could ensure their purity and therefore take steps toward protecting the lives of addicts who ingest impure drugs. In addition, he said, the drugs could be dispensed under a controlled environment through physicians' prescriptions or clinics. "I don't want to see it in grocery stores," he told reporters. "I'm assuming that wouldn't happen. The more dangerous the perception of the drug, the more control there would be." In fact, Jackson said he regards marijuana as less of a threat to public health than alcohol. He believed that if problem drinkers had access to marijuana it is likely they would use that drug instead of drinking heavily.

Finally, Jackson said, the government could raise billions of dollars in revenue by assessing taxes on drugs like marijuana, cocaine, and heroin. "Control it, regulate it, tax it," he said. "If you legalize it we might actually have a healthier society."

In Washington, D.C., officials reacted coolly to Jackson's ideas. Barry McCaffrey, who at the time was the head of the White House Office of National Drug Policy, said, "He's not listening to drug treatment experts and law enforcement authorities and educators in his own state about the devastation that these drugs do on Americans."

While governor of New Mexico, Gary Johnson argued that the federal government's "war on drugs" had been a failure, and he advocated the legalization of such drugs as marijuana, cocaine, and heroin.

# MEDICAL MARIJUANA

On most days, Angel Raich feels the need to smoke marijuana. Raich is by no means a pothead living on the fringes of society. Instead, she is the mother of two teenagers; her family lives in a comfortable home in Oakland, California.

Raich smokes marijuana because she lives with an inoperable brain tumor as well as scoliosis, a deformity of the spine. She started smoking marijuana in 1997 at the recommendation of her physician, who told her it would help ease her pain. The drug helped so much that she was able to walk again after spending two years in a wheelchair. "If I stop using it, I would die," Raich told reporters in 2005.

Raich is one of thousands of Americans who use marijuana for its medicinal, painkilling qualities. By 2005, eleven states, including Alaska, Arizona, California, Colorado, Hawaii, Maine, Montana, Nevada, Oregon, Vermont, and Washington, established laws permitting the use of "medical marijuana."

However, the federal government opposes the use of marijuana for any purposes, arguing that the 1970 federal law that declared marijuana a controlled substance takes precedence over all state laws. In 2002, the U.S. Justice Department started prosecuting marijuana growers who provide medical marijuana to patients. That action prompted Raich and another woman, Diane Monson of Oroville, California, to sue the Justice Department, contending that it is wrong for the federal government to cut off their access to medical marijuana. Monson suffers from a degenerative spine disease and grows marijuana plants in her backyard. Her

conducted in 2001, 77 percent of Americans oppose a federal law that would lower the drinking age to eighteen. The same poll found 60 percent of Americans in favor of even stricter laws governing underage drinking.

While a clear majority of Americans do not want to see the legal drinking age lowered, some political leaders and educators are nevertheless advocating that governments reassess their underage drinking laws and consider lowering the legal drinking age. They argue that laws do not prevent young people from drinking. A teenager who wants to drink will find a way to obtain alcoholic beverages — either by stealing a plants were seized in a raid by federal drug agents. (Raich's supply is provided by two anonymous "caregivers" who grow the plant secretly.)

Gallup polls show that Americans overwhelmingly support making medical marijuana available to people who need it. In 1999, a Gallup poll showed that 73 percent of Americans favor the legalization of marijuana in cases in which a physician has prescribed it to relieve pain and suffering. In contrast, a Gallup poll taken a year later showed just 31 percent of Americans favor legalization of marijuana for recreational purposes.

The lawsuit brought by Raich and Monson made its way through the federal courts and was finally argued before the U.S. Supreme Court in November 2004. The court took seven months to deliberate the issue, finally issuing a decision in June 2005. In a six to three decision, the Supreme Court refused to bar the Justice Department from prosecuting growers of medical marijuana. In the majority opinion, Justice John Paul Stevens sympathized with the plights of Raich and Monson, but insisted that there is too much danger of medical marijuana falling into the hands of recreational users. He wrote, "The likelihood that all such production . . . will precisely match the patients' medical needs . . . seems remote, whereas the danger that excesses will satisfy some of the admittedly enormous demand for recreational use seems obvious."

As for Raich, the California woman said she plans to defy the order of the court. "I do not have a choice but to continue using cannabis," she told reporters.

case of beer out of a neighbor's garage, breaking into his parents' liquor cabinet at home, or by making use of a fake identification card. Those who support lowering the legal drinking age contend that when young people must drink secretly, they learn bad habits—such as bingeing on alcohol or drinking and driving. Why not lower the drinking age to 18 so that older teenagers and young adults can drink in a legal environment under controlled circumstances, such as a bar, a restaurant, or at a family dinner? A group of teenagers who steal a case of beer will probably want to drain the whole case in one sitting, they argue, but if those same teenagers were able to legally enter a bar they might be satisfied with one or two beers. If it appeared they were drinking to excess, the bartender could refuse to serve them.

Peter Coors, who was elected to the U.S. Senate in 2004, has long advocated lowering the drinking age. The great-grandson of Adolph Coors, the founder of Coors Brewing—the third-largest brewery in America—Peter Coors says that his position on this issue is not to help his company sell more beer, but to teach young people how to drink legally and responsibly. He told a *USA Today* reporter in 1997:

> If you chug a gallon of alcohol, you're going to die. We ought to be telling kids that in school. We shouldn't be preaching, "Don't drink." We should be preaching responsible drinking. Maybe the answer is lowering the drinking age so that kids learn to be responsible about drinking at [a] younger age. I'm not an advocate of trying to get people to drink, but kids are drinking now anyway. All we've done is criminalize them. What I'd like to see this country do is to have a situation where kids could learn to drink responsibly over time, but there should be zero tolerance for aberrant behavior associated with alcohol. Zero tolerance for drinking and driving. Zero tolerance for crimes committed under the influence.

His thoughts have been echoed by Ruth C. Engs, an Indiana University professor. In a 1998 essay published in the academic journal *CQ Researcher*, she compared underage drinking laws to the failed "Noble Experiment" of the 1920s. "Although the legal purchase age is twenty-one years of age, a majority of college students under this age consume alcohol but in an irresponsible manner," Engs wrote. "This is because drinking by these youths is seen as an enticing 'forbidden fruit,' a 'badge of rebellion against authority' and a symbol of 'adulthood.'"

The Prohibition laws, Engs said, "were finally repealed because they were unenforceable and because the backlash towards them caused other social problems.

Today we are repeating history and making the same mistakes that occurred in the past. Prohibition did not work then and prohibition for young people under the age of twenty-one is not working now. . . . It behooves us as a nation to change our current prohibition law and to teach responsible drinking techniques for those who choose to consume alcoholic beverages."

On the other side of the argument are advocates for keeping the minimum legal drinking age exactly where it is. The group Mothers Against Drunk Driving reports that since the MLDA was raised to 21, highway fatalities involving young drinkers have been reduced by 13 percent. Overall, MADD says, raising the drinking age has saved an estimated 22,000 lives. According to a statement posted on MADD's website, "The passage of the twenty-one minimum drinking age law in 1984 was a large step forward for traffic safety and for underage drinking prevention. Now, we need to make sure that the law is enforced and effective."

In fact, MADD argues, people who are 21 or in their early twenties aren't very responsible drinkers, either. According to statistics compiled by the organization for 2003, in accidents that resulted in fatalities the drivers most likely to be intoxicated were between the ages of 21 and 24. The statistics show that 32 percent of drivers between the ages of 21 and 24 involved in fatal car crashes had blood alcohol levels above 0.08.

Two young people stagger home after having too much to drink. Although some organizations are in favor of lowering the legal drinking age, most people believe 18-year-olds lack the maturity to drink responsibly.

## AGE DISCRIMINATION?

Although lowering the minimum drinking age remains a politically unpopular idea, there are some groups that lobby lawmakers in the hopes that the drinking laws

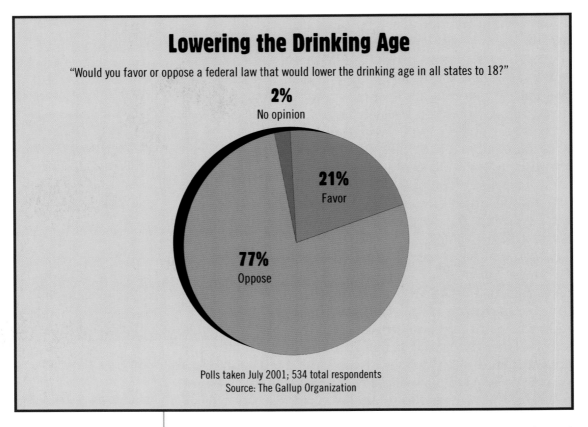

## Lowering the Drinking Age

"Would you favor or oppose a federal law that would lower the drinking age in all states to 18?"

**2%**
No opinion

**21%**
Favor

**77%**
Oppose

Polls taken July 2001; 534 total respondents
Source: The Gallup Organization

will one day be liberalized. The Washington-based National Youth Rights Association raises many of the same points that returning veterans of the Vietnam War raised in the 1960s and 1970s: People as young as 18 vote, pay taxes, and serve in the military. Why can't they also enjoy a legal drink? Alex Koroknay-Palicz, the president of the association, says, "It's just an absolutely twisted double standard to say that somebody is mature and responsible enough to drive a tank through Baghdad, and absurd to say they are not mature enough to have a glass of wine or can of beer."

There are a few places where people under age 21 can drink legally, such as aboard cruise ships. Starting in 2002, several cruise lines lowered their drinking ages to 18, although when the ships are within territorial waters of the United States the bars close to anyone under the age of 21.

In Vermont during 2005, lawmakers proposed lowering the state's drinking age to 18. Proponents said they realized the state would lose as much as $9.7 million a year in federal highway grants, but they suggested that the lost revenue could be made up by increased taxes collected on the sales of beer, wine, and liquor. The bill lowering the Vermont drinking age was proposed by Richard C. Marron, a state representative. A short time after Marron introduced the bill, 17 legislators signed on as cosponsors. To become law, the bill would have to be approved by the full membership of the Vermont Legislature and signed by Governor Jim

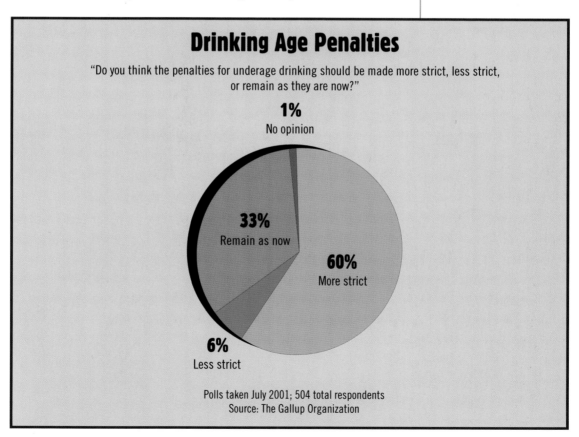

## Drinking Age Penalties

"Do you think the penalties for underage drinking should be made more strict, less strict, or remain as they are now?"

**1%**
No opinion

**33%**
Remain as now

**60%**
More strict

**6%**
Less strict

Polls taken July 2001; 504 total respondents
Source: The Gallup Organization

Douglas, whose spokesman, Jason Gibbs, told reporters that it was unlikely the governor would sign the bill because he feared loss of federal highway money. Still, as reported in a 2005 *New York Times* article, Gibbs said, "Philosophically, it's difficult to reconcile the notion that you can enlist in the military, serve your country, go to war, but not go into your local pub and get a draft beer."

Ronald D. Liebowitz, the president of Middlebury College in Vermont, said that back in the 1970s and early 1980s—when the drinking age was still 18—there were always young people who drank too much. Still, he said, the binge drinking of today is often out of

Many young people find ways to drink alcohol despite laws prohibiting drinking by people under age 21.

control. He said, "You had kids drinking beer and getting sick on beer, but you didn't have gross alcohol poisoning and binge drinking" that many young people fall victim to today.

Representative Marron suggested that a law banning alcohol sales to an eighteen-year-old customer might also be considered a form of age discrimination. He said, "Now we have a legal age of eighteen to do everything else, but you can't drink until you're twenty-one. I'm not pushing it to the level of it being unconstitutional, but I do think it's a form of age discrimination. If we did something else, like said you couldn't use a public campsite until you're twenty-one, we would have an equal-protection-of-laws issue."

# 6

# ENHANCING PERFORMANCE

**B**abe Ruth's record of 60 home runs hit in a single season stood for decades as one of baseball's most important records. After Ruth set the record in 1927, a few sluggers came close to the mark—Jimmie Fox of the old Philadelphia Athletics and Hank Greenberg of the Detroit Tigers each hit 58 homers in a season, and Hack Wilson of the Chicago Cubs knocked in 56—but Ruth's record of 60 seemed to be an unreachable peak, destined to last forever.

As the 1961 baseball season got underway, two sluggers for the New York Yankees, Roger Maris and Mickey Mantle, started chasing Ruth's record in a competition that transfixed the nation's baseball fans. For nearly six months, fans followed the Yankee sluggers as they chased Ruth's elusive record. Finally, in the fourth inning in a game against the Boston Red Sox on October 1—the last day of the season—Roger Maris hit his 61st home run, setting a new record. Mantle, who had been ill and unable to play for the final few games of the season, finished with 54.

Roger Maris's single-season home run mark would prove to be just as hard to break as the

(Opposite) Baseball stars Jose Canseco, Sammy Sosa, Mark McGwire, Rafael Palmeiro, and Curt Schilling listen to testimony during a March 2005 House Committee session on steroids. All were called to testify before the committee.

record set by Babe Ruth. In fact, it would be 37 years before Maris's record was broken—three years longer than it had taken to smash Ruth's mark of 60. But in 1998, two sluggers, Mark McGwire of the St. Louis Cardinals and Sammy Sosa of the Chicago Cubs, set the National League on fire as they put on a season-long home run derby. Even casual baseball fans could not help but be drawn in by the competition put on that summer by McGwire and Sosa. That June, a Gallup poll reported that 73 percent of baseball fans believed Maris's record would be broken that year. As it turned out, both men would break the record—McGwire hit 70 homers in 1998 while Sosa slugged 66. But McGwire's record would last just three years. In 2001 Barry Bonds of the San Francisco Giants hit 73 homers.

One could hardly dispute that those were incredible accomplishments, but soon many people who followed baseball wanted to know how the records of Ruth and Maris, which had held up for decades, were suddenly broken by so many players. What's more, the records were not merely broken—they were obliterated. Sosa, for example, hit more than 60 homers in three straight seasons. It was not just a few prodigious home-run hitters either: before the mid-1990s, it had been rare for a player to hit 50 home runs in a season. By 2001, several players were surpassing that mark each season.

Alas, when the answer became apparent, few people could say they were surprised.

## NOT A GOOD DAY FOR BASEBALL

Seven years after McGwire and Sosa broke Maris's record, both men found themselves sitting uncomfortably before the U.S. House Government Reform Committee, which had convened in Washington, D.C., to investigate charges that steroid abuse in baseball had grown into epidemic proportions. Along with Sosa and McGwire, among the witnesses called to testify was retired player Jose Canseco, who had written a book acknowledging that he had used steroids during the course of a career in which he hit 462 home runs. In his book, *Juiced: Wild Times, Rampant 'Roids, Smash Hits, and How Baseball Got Big*, Canseco claimed he injected McGwire with steroids while the two men were teammates on the Oakland Athletics. Canseco also wrote in the book that he knew Sosa used steroids. Another player accused of taking steroids by Canseco, Rafael Palmeiro, was also called to testify.

Sosa—who was once suspended for cheating by using a corked bat in a game—flatly denied the charge that he used steroids. In a statement read to the House committee, Sosa said, "Everything I have heard about steroids and human growth hormones is that they are very bad for you, even lethal. I would never put anything dangerous like that in my body. Nor would I encourage other people to use illegal performance-enhancing drugs." Palmeiro also denied taking performance-enhancing drugs. "I have never used steroids. Period," he said.

But McGwire refused to answer questions about steroid abuse, choosing to invoke his rights under the Fifth Amendment to the U.S. Constitution, which protects citizens against self-incrimination. "I'm not here to discuss the past," the retired slugger told the House committee. "I'm here to be positive about this subject." When committee members pressed him to disclose whether he

Retired baseball player Jose Canseco poses with his book *Juiced*, in which he admitted to using anabolic steroids during his career and claimed other players did so also. Canseco's book caused a national controversy, and led to the Congressional hearings on steroid use in baseball.

Barry Bonds, pictured in 1986 and 2005, had long been suspected of using steroids to dramatically increase his muscle mass and strength. He denied the accusations until he was implicated in the BALCO doping scandal.

had used steroids, McGwire said, "Like I said earlier, I'm not going to go into the past and talk about my past. . . . I've accepted my attorneys' advice not to comment on this issue."

It was not a good day for baseball. Some of the game's most popular players were now suspected of using steroids to make themselves stronger and faster so they could hit more home runs. The hearings left a black cloud hanging over the 1998 McGwire-Sosa home-run chase and the accomplishments of Barry Bonds, causing many people to wonder whether their home-run records should be invalidated. After all, players who took performance-enhancing drugs were cheating. After the congressional hearing, baseball historian Bill James told *Newsweek* magazine, "I certainly think that McGwire's Hall of Fame candidacy is damaged."

Although Bonds had not appeared at the hearing, his record-setting performances were also called into question. After denying for years that he had taken performance-enhancing drugs that helped turn his thin and wiry frame into the body of a beefy slugger, Bond's name surfaced as a grand jury investigated a steroid supply ring in the San Francisco area known as the Bay Area Laboratory Cooperative, or BALCO. Finally, Bonds admitted taking the substances, but claimed he did not know he had been injecting himself with steroids. Most people did not believe his story. In 2005, a Gallup poll reported that 42 percent of respondents believed Bonds was probably not telling the truth, while 33 percent believed he was definitely not telling the truth.

## THE EDGE

Steroids, as well as another class of drugs known as human growth hormones, are illegal in the United States without a prescription, but in Mexico and other Latin American countries they can be purchased off the shelves of many pharmacies. That has led traffickers to obtain the drugs in Latin America and smuggle them into the United States, where they are sold to professional athletes, college players, bodybuilders, and even high school athletes. Unlike other drugs, steroids do not provide their users with a hazy, narcotic high that gives them feelings of euphoria or distorted, mind-twisting psychedelic hallucinations. Steroids and human growth hormones help build up muscle mass and can enhance athletic performance. Once in the body, steroids will be converted into the male hormone testosterone, which helps the body convert protein into muscle mass. Doctors prescribe steroids to patients whose bodies do not produce enough testosterone, the result of which can cause stunted growth, delayed puberty, impotence, and infertility. In addition, AIDS patients who lose muscle mass because of their disease are often prescribed steroids.

The typical male body produces about ten milligrams of testosterone a day. Athletes who take steroids often consume doses that will help them produce hundreds of milligrams. By taking such massive doses, athletes can expect to see quick results to their training. Within weeks, they will be stronger and faster.

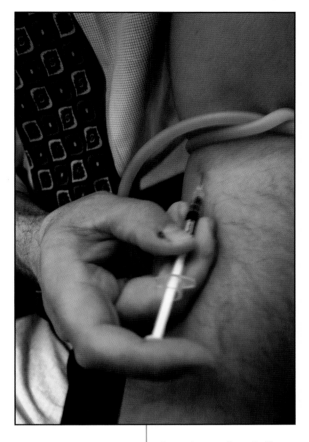

Some types of anabolic steroids help the user's body develop greater muscle mass, while others enable the user to recover more quickly after strenuous workouts. However, all steroids produce dangerous and sometimes life-threatening side effects.

However, the side effects will soon start manifesting themselves as well.

After steroid use begins, the body stops producing its own testosterone. The glands that produce testosterone—the testicles—start shrinking and could eventually lose all their ability to produce testosterone. That could lead to a lower sperm count, which could make the steroid user infertile. Therefore, male steroid users take the risk of losing their ability to become fathers. Women who take steroids may lose their hair or grow hair in the wrong places or experience menstrual abnormalities. Other side effects of steroid use include: bloating, weight gain, blood-clotting disorders, liver damage, premature heart attacks and stroke, high cholesterol, weak tendons, high blood pressure, addiction dependence, acne, kidney problems, cancer, and personality disorders known as "Roid Rage."

Human growth hormones present their own dangers. Athletes take them to strengthen their joints. One of the side effects is an enlarged head. Baseball players who have taken human growth hormones say they have difficulty getting their batting helmets to stay on. Facial characteristics also change, as brows and jaws become more pronounced.

Athletes who take steroids and human growth hormones tend to sustain muscle and bone injuries more often than athletes who do not take performance-enhancing drugs. They also cause physical problems after an athlete's playing days end. In 1992, former football star Lyle Alzado died of brain cancer. He believed his disease was caused by excessive steroid use during his playing career. When he died, Alzado was 43 years old. And in 2004, former National League Most Valuable Player Ken Caminiti died of a heart attack. In a *Sports Illustrated* article published two years before his death, Caminiti admitted that he had used steroids in 1996, his MVP year. He was just 41 years old when he died.

In the *Sports Illustrated* article, Caminiti estimated that half of all Major League baseball players use steroids. "If a young player were to ask me what to do, I'm not going to tell him it's bad," Caminiti told the magazine. "Look at all the money in the game: You have a chance to set your family up, to get your daughter into a better school. . . . So I can't say, 'Don't do it,' when the guy next to you is as big as a house and he's going to take your job and make the money." Added author David Callahan, in his 2004 book *The Cheating Culture*:

> Even the best players at the top of baseball are anxious to keep their position. Maybe Sammy Sosa didn't purposely bring a corked bat into the game in June 2003, as he has claimed. And maybe Sosa doesn't use steroids as is widely rumored. But if he did these things it wouldn't be that surprising: As a slugger like Sosa gets older,

Football player Lyle Alzado, pictured with his wife, contracted fatal brain cancer which he believed was a result of steroid abuse.

Not all steroid abusers are trying to enhance their athletic performance. Some teenage girls experiment with steroids in order to lose weight and tone their bodies.

it's harder for him to sustain the muscle and power needed to drive balls over the fence and justify his multimillion-dollar salary. It's natural to look for an edge in this kind of situation.

Teenagers who take steroids face a unique set of medical issues. If they start taking steroids while their bodies are still developing, their bones might stop developing on their own, leaving them shorter than their peers. Steroid use in teens has also led to mental illness.

Young athletes who hope to win scholarships to big-time college sports programs and pursue professional sports careers have been known to experiment with steroids. In recent years, many high school athletic departments have required student athletes to take regular drug tests. But a troubling study released in 2005 by Oregon Health and Science University found that many teenage girls who have no interest in athletics had also started experimenting with steroids. The reason? The girls wanted to obtain the toned look of supermodels and movie stars.

The study found that two-thirds of Oregon high school girls who admitted taking steroids are not athletes. What's more, the researchers learned that many girls who take steroids have already tried other dangerous ways of getting thin—such as abusing laxatives to purge their bodies of weight and diuretics to purge their bodies of water. Other school officials also said they have noticed young girls turning more and more to steroids. Said Rutgers University counselor Jeff Hoerger in a

2005 Associated Press story, "With young women, you see them using it more as a weight control and body fat reduction method."

## THE RESPONSE OF PRO SPORTS LEAGUES

The steroid allegations that were raised at the 2005 House committee hearings did not come as a surprise to people who followed sports. Steroid use has long been alleged in many forms of athletic competition, and officials of the various major league sports associations have responded in varying degrees to the crisis. Some of their responses have been tough, some have been lenient, and some have chosen not to respond at all. For example, the National Basketball Association's policy includes a five-game suspension for first-time offenders, while the National Hockey League suspends first-time violaters of its drug policy for 20 games, although NHL critics claim the drug tests do not occur often enough.

One of the tougher policies in sports is followed by the National Football League, which in the late 1980s recognized the growing problem of steroid use among players. In 1989, the NFL instituted random testing for steroids. Players who are found to have used steroids face mandatory four-game suspensions for their first offense, six-game suspensions for the second offense, and season-long suspensions for the third offense. Since the NFL's policy was initiated, 54 players have been disciplined after they tested positive for steroids.

Still, members of the House Government Reform Committee, which also heard testimony from NFL officials at the 2005 hearings, suspected that some football players continue to use steroids. Asked U.S. Representative Tom Davis, "How is the average American supposed to look at the size, strength, and speed of today's NFL linebackers and not conclude that they might be taking performance-enhancing drugs?"

As for baseball's steroid policy, league officials instituted a minimal testing program in 2002 that critics said

Following admonitions from the House Government Reform Committee, Major League Baseball commissioner Bud Selig proposed tougher penalties for steroid offenses.

hardly addressed the issue. Following the 2004 season, Major League baseball instituted a 10-day suspension for first offenders. Shortly before the start of the 2005 season, four players were handed suspensions. Nevertheless, at the conclusion of the congressional hearings, members of the House Government Reform Committee warned baseball officials that if they do not clean up their sport, Congress would write a law imposing heavy fines and suspensions on athletes. Congressman Henry Waxman, a member of the committee, said, "America is asking baseball for integrity. An unequivocal statement against cheating. An unimpeachable policy. And a reason for all of us to have faith in the sport again."

In an effort to set a uniform steroid policy for the major professional leagues in the United States, members of Congress introduced the Clean Sports Act in the spring of 2005. The bill called for professional athletes to be subject to a two-year ban for a first positive drug test. "There's got to be some kind of legislation that will absolutely test and punish professional athletes that use performance-enhancing drugs," one of the bill's sponsors, Senator John McCain of Arizona, told the Associated Press. "There are a lot of issues we would much rather address. And if the professional leagues had taken action, we would not be here today. But they have not taken sufficient action."

In response, baseball Commissioner Bud Selig proposed a tougher testing program. He asked the Major League Baseball Players Association (MLBPA)—the union that represents the players—to accept a tough new policy that would include a 50-game suspension for the first offense, 100-game suspension for the second offense, and a lifetime ban on third-time offenders. "Third offenders should be banned permanently," Selig said in a letter to union officials. "I recognize the need for progressive discipline, but a third-time offender has no place in the game. Steroid users cheat the game. After three offenses, they have no place in it."

Although some players and union leaders were initially cool toward Selig's plan, saying that the old steroids testing program should be given a chance before it was replaced with a tougher program, pressure ultimately forced the union to give in to the new proposal. In November 2005, the MLBPA agreed to the tougher steroid testing plan, along with a proposal under which players would be regularly tested for amphetamine use. (Some players use amphetamines to provide extra energy during the long baseball season.) The tougher policy was praised by congressional leaders involved in the steroid hearings. "The agreement reached between Major League Baseball and the Players Association is the type of self-initiated action we were hoping for all along," said U.S. Representative Tom Davis, chairman of the House Government Reform Committee. "While the new policy is not what it would be had I authored it, it is a much stronger policy, one with multiple random tests and far tougher penalties for even first-time offenders."

## "RUINING THE GAME"

While members of Congress, baseball players, and league officials fretted over what to do about baseball's steroids problem, baseball fans made it clear that they wanted performance-enhancing drugs out of the sport.

According to a Gallup poll conducted shortly after the conclusion of the House Government Reform Committee hearings, 40 percent of respondents believe

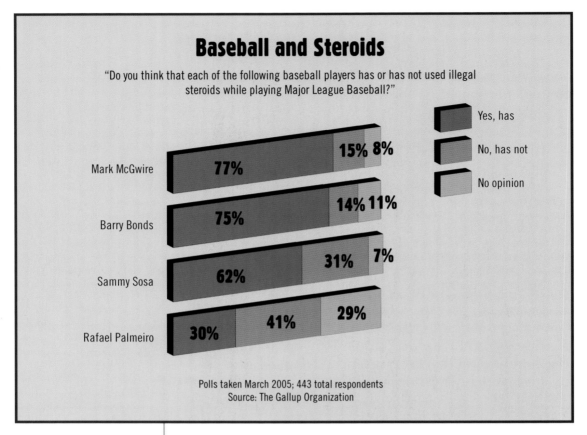

## Baseball and Steroids

"Do you think that each of the following baseball players has or has not used illegal steroids while playing Major League Baseball?"

Yes, has
No, has not
No opinion

Mark McGwire: 77% — 15% — 8%
Barry Bonds: 75% — 14% — 11%
Sammy Sosa: 62% — 31% — 7%
Rafael Palmeiro: 30% — 41% — 29%

Polls taken March 2005; 443 total respondents
Source: The Gallup Organization

that performance-enhancing drugs "are ruining the game" of baseball. What's more, the fans said the 1998 home run race between McGwire and Sosa has now been tainted by the steroid allegations, and that Bonds' record of 73 homers in a season can also be called into question. Said a Gallup analysis:

> The Gallup survey found most fans believe McGwire would likely have tested positive for steroids had a testing program been in place during his career. More than three out of four baseball fans [77 percent] now believe McGwire used steroids despite his repeated denials during his career. In addition, only 53 percent of American adults have a favorable opinion of McGwire now, compared with 87 percent in a December 1998 Gallup poll following his record-setting season.

Sammy Sosa and Rafael Palmeiro, two other players implicated by Jose Canseco, both flatly denied any steroid use during their testimony before the committee. However, in March baseball fans were more likely to believe Palmeiro than Sosa. Sixty-two percent of fans believed Sosa had used steroids, compared with 30 percent for Palmeiro. But Palmeiro's credibility was dealt a major blow when he failed a steroid test and served a 10-game suspension during August 2005. As with McGwire, the public's opinion of Sosa has also been damaged—falling from 83 percent favorable in December 1998 to 55 percent in the March Gallup poll.

The only player not in the hearing room who might have been able to add to the discussion was Barry Bonds of the San Francisco Giants—accused by many of being the poster boy for steroid abuse. Bonds testified in 2003 before a federal grand jury investigating the BALCO Laboratories steroid case, and according to records leaked to a San Francisco newspaper, denied that he knowingly used steroids allegedly supplied by his personal trainer, who is one of four people facing criminal charges in the case. Although Bonds is just the third player in baseball history to hit more than 700 home runs, 75 percent of baseball fans believe at least some of those homers were hit with the aid of steroids or other performance-enhancing drugs.

Clearly, steroid use has cost some baseball players and other athletes their lives. It may cost McGwire, Sosa, Palmeiro, and Bonds election to the Hall of Fame. It has left a dark cloud hanging over one of the sports world's most valued records. And, perhaps, it has cost baseball the support of some fans. According to the March 2005 poll, 39 percent of Americans regard themselves as baseball fans—a 4 percent drop over a similar poll taken in December 2004, before the House Government Reform Committee convened its hearings.

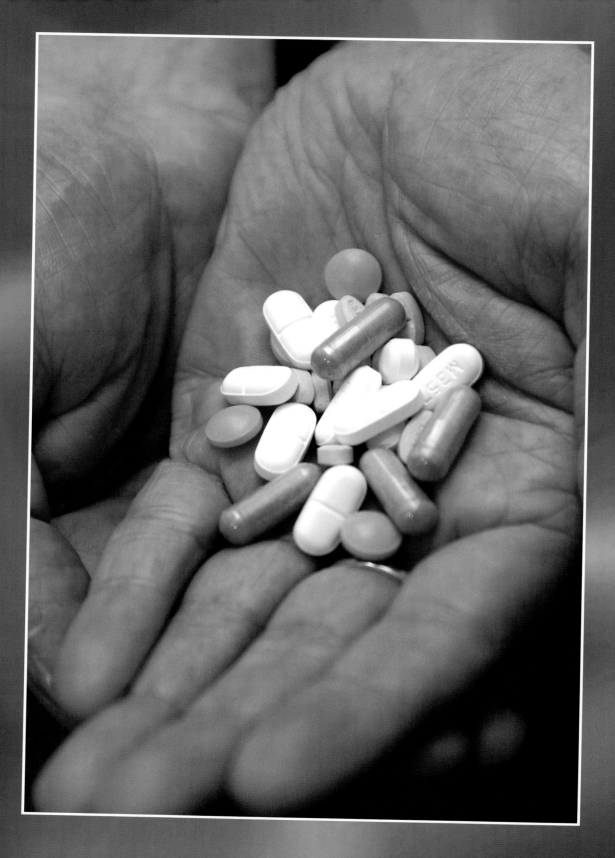

# 7

# THE RESPONSIBILITY OF PARENTS

**M**any Americans develop their drinking and drug habits as teenagers—a fact that is confirmed by Gallup polls. In 2005, 17 percent of teenagers as young as 13 told a Gallup poll they have consumed alcohol and 13 percent said they have tried marijuana. Whereas it can be argued that drug and drinking habits by parents influence young people, even parents who take precautions to shield their children from exposure to substances may find out they are not doing enough.

In 2005 the advocacy group Partnership for a Drug Free America released a study showing a new trend in drug abuse among young people: many are abusing their parents' prescription painkillers, often popping pills right out of the bottles that are in the bathroom medicine cabinets. Said Partnership Chairman Roy Bostock, "A new category of substance abuse is emerging in America: Increasingly, teenagers are getting high through the intentional abuse of medications. For the first time, our national study finds that today's teens are more likely to have abused a prescription painkiller to get high than they

In a dangerous new trend, young people are getting high using prescription medications, such as painkillers and cough syrups.

**99**

are to have experimented with a variety of illicit drugs—including ecstasy, cocaine, crack and LSD."

During the 1990s, the abuse of prescription painkillers surfaced in the drug culture. For example, the development of the painkiller OxyContin was regarded as a significant breakthrough in managing the pain of cancer patients. Until the development of OxyContin, most painkillers lasted a few hours, meaning the patient had to continually take pills for relief from pain. But OxyContin's developers found a way to provide the painkilling effects of the drug through a time-release formula, meaning the numbing agents were released into the bloodstream over the course of a full day. Now, the patient could be free from pain with a minimum of doses.

It did not take long for drug abusers to find a way to beat the time-release feature of the pill. Simply by smashing the pill or chewing it, drug abusers found they could receive the full hit of the narcotic at once, thereby rewarding themselves with a high similar to what they could obtain through an injection of heroin. Today, OxyContin is a commonly abused drug. Pharmacies are often burglarized by drug abusers anxious to get their hands on the pills. Many drug users also try to fake pain so that doctors will prescribe the pills, or they steal prescription pads and attempt to forge OxyContin prescriptions for themselves.

According to statistics released by the Partnership, 2.3 million teenagers in the United States are believed to be abusing OxyContin each year. Another painkillers abused by young people is Vicodin. Some young people also abuse Ritalin, a stimulant that helps people suffering from Attention Deficit Disorder (ADD) stay focused. Drug abusers who swallow Ritalin hope to gain the energetic high similar to what they would feel through a dose of speed or crystal meth.

Over-the-counter medications are also widely abused by young people, the Partnership said. Cough medications containing dextromethorphan (DXM) are typically abused. By drinking large quantities of dextromethorphan, drug abusers are often rewarded with a hallucinatory effect. "Adolescent abuse of prescription and over-the-counter medications represents one of the most significant developments in substance abuse trends in recent memory," said Steve Pasierb, president of the Partnership. "Educating parents and teenagers about the risks of abusing medications will be exceptionally challenging, but it clearly must be done."

Illicit drugs such as ecstasy (top) are still in use today. But teenagers are also likely to abuse prescription drugs, including the painkiller OxyContin (bottom).

The Partnership's research has been confirmed by other sources. In 2004, a Gallup poll reported that 53 percent of teens between the ages of 13 and 17 "see abuse of legal, over-the-counter remedies such as cold medicine, recently identified as a growing trend among teens, as a very serious or somewhat serious health issue among their peers." Meanwhile, in late 2004, the annual *Monitoring the Future* study, a project conducted by the University of Michigan to assess substance abuse patterns among young people, also found the abuse of prescription drugs, particularly OxyContin, on the rise among teenagers. The *Monitoring the Future* study found that use of OxyContin rose from 1.3 percent of all eighth-graders in 2002 to 1.7 percent of eighth-graders in 2004, while use of the drug by tenth-graders rose from 3 percent in 2002 to 3.5 percent in 2004. Students in the twelfth grade showed the steepest rise in OxyContin use. The *Monitoring the Future* study showed use by students in that age group rose by a full point over the two-year period, from 4 percent in 2002 to 5 percent in 2004. Said Lloyd Johnston, the principal investigator for the *Monitoring the Future* study, "Considering the addictive potential of this drug, which is a powerful synthetic narcotic used to control pain, we think that these are disturbingly high rates of involvement by American young people."

## TALKING OVER PROBLEMS

It could be argued that parents could do a lot to prevent their children from trying drugs and alcohols if they simply talked frankly to them about substance abuse and paid closer attention to their habits. And yet, a Gallup poll in 2003 found that few families eat dinner together — typically the best time to talk over problems. The poll reported that just 28 percent of American families with children eat together seven nights a week, while 47 percent of families eat together between four and six evenings a week, and 24 percent of American families eat together three days or less each week. What is particularly troubling about the Gallup statistic is that it shows the number of families who make time to eat together every night of the week is on the decline. In 2001, a similar poll found that 38 percent of American families with children eat together seven nights a week. Said a Gallup analysis:

> All parents want to know what's going on with their children, but a 2003 study by the National Center on Addiction and Substance Abuse at Columbia University suggests that family dinners can have some concrete benefits for teenagers. The study found that teens who have dinner with their families two nights a week or less are twice as likely to take drugs, more likely to be "high stress," more likely to say they are often bored, and less likely to perform well in school than teens who eat with their families five to seven times a week.

Parents may be able to do much in the way of alerting young people about the dangers of misusing prescription and over-the-counter drugs as well as the other substance-abuse threats that have surfaced in recent years. With alcohol use widespread among teenagers, with high school athletes experimenting with

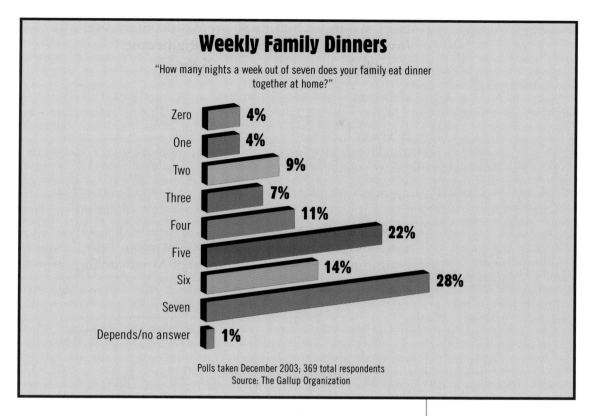

**Weekly Family Dinners**

"How many nights a week out of seven does your family eat dinner together at home?"

- Zero — 4%
- One — 4%
- Two — 9%
- Three — 7%
- Four — 11%
- Five — 22%
- Six — 14%
- Seven — 28%
- Depends/no answer — 1%

Polls taken December 2003; 369 total respondents
Source: The Gallup Organization

steroids, and with old foes such as marijuana, methamphetamine, heroin, and LSD always within reach, experts agree that any message of warning that hits a young person's ears is worth sending. Indeed, there is no question that many adults learned their drinking and drug abusing habits as teenagers. But the evidence also shows that the teenage years are also the best years to learn about the dangers of drinking and drug abuse, and parents would do well to reach out to their children with straightforward and frank advice.

**binge drinking**—unrestrained and often excessive indulgence with alcohol consumption. SAMHSA defines binge drinking for men as drinking five or more alcoholic drinks in quick succession; for women, the definition is four drinks.

**breweries**—factories in which beer is manufactured.

**caffeine**—ingredient in coffee, tea, and some soft drinks that works as a stimulant.

**cartel**—an organization formed to control prices and trade of a specific product (e.g., cocaine).

**decriminalize**—to remove or reduce the criminal classification or status of; to repeal a strict ban on while keeping under some form of regulation.

**depression**—in economics, a period in which business, employment and the value of investments decline.

**distillers**—manufacturers of gin, whiskey, and other forms of hard liquor.

**ecstasy**—a synthetic drug (3-4-methylenedioxymethamphetamine, or MDMA) that produces hallucinations as well as a narcotic effect similar to amphetamines.

**hashish**—flowers and leaves of the Indian hemp plant that provide a narcotic effect when smoked.

**hormones**—chemicals manufactured by the body that affect the functions of specific organs.

**huffing**—the sniffing/inhaling through one's mouth of a household or commercial product (e.g., lighter fluids, cleaning solutions, gasoline, paint, glue) for the purpose of experiencing an intoxicating effect.

**jaundice**—buildup of bile in the blood that causes skin and whites of eyes to turn yellow; often accompanied by loss of appetite and fatigue.

**patent medicines**—medications sold without a prescription in the 1800s and early 1900s.

**stills**—devices used to distill alcoholic beverages.

**temperance**—abstinence from consumption of alcoholic beverages.

**toluene**—solvent added to glue to quicken drying time.

Gahlinger, Paul M. *Illegal Drugs: A Complete Guide to Their History, Chemistry, Use and Abuse*. Las Vegas, N.V., Sagebrush Press, 2001.

Kuhn, Cynthia, and others. *Buzzed: The Straight Facts about the Most Used and Abused Drugs from Alcohol to Ecstasy*. New York: W. W. Norton & Co., 2003.

Landry, Mim J. *Understanding Drugs of Abuse: The Processes of Addiction, Treatment, and Recovery*. Arlington, Va.: American Psychiatric Association; 1993.

Leone, Bruno, ed. *The War on Drugs: Opposing Viewpoints*. San Diego: Greenhaven Press, 1998.

Long, Robert Emmet, ed. *Drugs in America*. New York: H.W. Wilson Co., 1993.

Mogil, Cindy R. *Swallowing a Bitter Pill: How Prescription and Over-The-Counter Drug Abuse Is Ruining Lives—My Story*. Far Hills, N.J.: New Horizon Press. 2001.

Zailckas, Koren. *Smashed: Story of a Drunken Girlhood*. New York: Viking Adult, 2005.

# BIBLIOGRAPHY

## BOOKS AND PERIODICALS

"Baseball on the Hot Seat: Excerpts from House Committee Hearing on Steroids," *Los Angeles Times*, March 18, 2005.

Blizzard, Rick. "Americans and Alcohol: Drink, Drank, Drunk?" Gallup Organization, August 24, 2004.

Blum, Ronald. "Selig Seeks 50-Game Penalty for Steroids," Associated Press, April 30, 2005.

Brecher, Edward M. *Licit and Illicit Drugs*. Mount Vernon, N.Y.: Consumers Union, 1972.

Burns, Eric. *The Spirits of America: A Social History of Alcohol*. Philadelphia: Temple University Press, 2004.

Callahan, David. *The Cheating Culture*. New York: Harcourt, 2004.

Canseco, Jose. *Juiced: Wild Times, Rampant 'Roids, Smash Hits, and How Baseball Got Big*. New York: Regan Books, 2005.

Carlson, Darren K. "How Many Teens Say They've Driven Drunk?" Gallup Organization, March 22, 2005.

Elliot, Stuart. "Liquor Industry Ends Its Ad Ban in Broadcasting," *New York Times*, November 11, 1996.

Fendrich, Howard. "NFL Testifies on Sterioid Issue," Associated Press, April 28, 2005.

Ford, Peter. "Europe Shifts Out of Drug-War Mode," *Christian Science Monitor*, March 12, 2001.

Gallup, George. "Public Opposed to Legalizing Marijuana; Opinions Differ Sharply by Age, Region," Gallup poll, October 23, 1969.

Gillespie, Mark. "Baseball Fans Have Little Patience for Steroid Abuse," Gallup Organization, March 28, 2005.

Gosch, Martin A., and Richard Hammer. *The Last Testament of Lucky Luciano*. Boston: Little, Brown and Company, 1974.

Kohut, Andrew, and Larry Hugick. "Twenty Years After Woodstock, Era Gets Mixed Reviews; Liberal Views of Drugs Deplored, More Equality for Women Applauded," Gallup Poll News Service, August 7, 1989.

Johnson, Linda A. "Steroid Use on Rise Among Girls," Associated Press, April 26, 2005.

"L.I. Youths Inhale Glue in Model Kits For Narcotic Effect," *New York Times*, October 6, 1961.

Lyons, Linda. "Brains, Brawn or Beauty? Many Teens Choose 'Smart' Route," Gallup Organization, April 16, 2002.

———. "Americans Remain Opposed to Legalizing Marijuana," Gallup Organization, December 2, 2003.

———. "Drug Use Still Among Americans' Top Worries," Gallup Organization, April 5, 2005.

"Marijuana Arrests for Year 2003 Hit Record High, FBI Report Reveals," National Organization for Reform of Marijuana Laws news release, October 25, 2004.

Mason, Heather. "Empty Seats: Fewer Families Eat Together," Gallup Organization, January 20, 2004.

McMurray, Colleen. "Youth Survey: Alcohol and Drug Abuse Among Teens," Gallup Organization, April 6, 2004.

"Millions of Teens Report Using Rx and OTC Meds Without a Doctor's Order," Partnership for a Drug Free America news release, April 21, 2005.

Ness, Eliot. *The Untouchables*. New York: Pocket Books, 1987.

"Overall Teen Drug Use Continues Gradual Decline; But Use of Inhalants Rises," University of Michigan news release, December 21, 2004.

Simmons, Wendy W. "One in Six Americans Admit to Drinking Too Much," Gallup Organization, December 4, 2000.

Starr, Mark, and Eve Conant. "A Major League Mess," *Newsweek*, vol. 145, no. 13, March 28, 2005.

Thompson, Hunter S. *Fear and Loathing in Las Vegas and Other American Stories*. New York: Modern Library, 1996.

Verducci, Tom, and Don Yaeger. "Totally Juiced," *Sports Illustrated*, June 3, 2002, reprinted in David Callahan, *The Cheating Culture*. New York: Harcourt, 2004.

Wells, Melanie. "Coors Chief: Consider Lower Drinking Age," *USA Today*, September 10, 1997.

Wilson, Duff. "McGwire Offers No Denials at Steroid Hearings," *New York Times*, March 18, 2005.

Young-Witzel, Gyvel, and Michael Karl Witzel. *The Sparkling Story of Coca-Cola*. Stillwater, Minn.: Voyageur Press, 2002.

## INTERNET PUBLICATIONS

Belluck, Pam. "Vermont Considers Lowering Drinking Age to 18," *New York Times*, April 13, 2005, www.nytimes.com/2005/04/13/national/13drink.html

Engs, Ruth C. "Why the Drinking Age Should be Lowered: An Opinion Based on Research," *CQ Researcher*, March 20, 1998, available online at www.indiana.edu/~engs/articles.cqoped.

"Glen Campbell's Unique DWI Excuse," CBSNews.com, www.cbsnews.com/stories/2004/07/01/entertainment/main627135.shtml

"Lautenschlager : This Will Not Happen Again," WISC-TV, February 25, 2004, www.channel3000.com/news/2874942/detail.html

Miller, Carl H. "Beer and Television: Perfectly Tuned In," www.beerhistory.com/library/holdings/beer_commercials.shtml

"New Mexico Governor Calls for Legalizing Drugs," www.cnn.com/US/9910/06/legalizing.drugs.01/

"NPR's Interview with Armstrong Biographer Laurence Bergreen," www.npr.org/programs/specials/hotter/interview.html

Nufeld, Sara, and Laura Barnhardt. "Olympian Phelps Charged with Drunken Driving," *Baltimore Sun*, November 9, 2004, www.baltimoresun.com/sports/olympics/balte.md.phelps09nov09,1,5538706.story?coll=bal-sports-olympics&ctrack=2&cset=true

Rathke, Lisa. "Campaign is on to Lower Drinking Age," Associated Press, March 30, 2005, www.rutlandherald.com/apps/pbcs.dll/article?AID=/20050330/NEWS/50329005&SearchID=73207163075469

Thirty Years of America's Drug War, Frontline, www.pbs.org/wgbh/pages/frontline/shows/drugs/cron/

Turner, Brad. "Pot Activists Gather for Annual 420 Event, Authorities Show Restraint at CU," *Longmont Daily Times-Call*, April 21, 2005, www.longmontfyi.com/Local-Story.asp?id=1382


**REPORTS**

*Communication Strategy Guide: A Look at Methamphetamine Use Among Three Populations.* Rockville, M.D.: U.S. Substance Abuse and Mental Health Services Administration, 2000.

*Crimes of Indiscretion: Marijuana Arrests in the United States.* Washington: National Organization for Reform of Marijuana Laws, 2005.

"Drug and Human Performance Fact Sheet: Cannabis/Marijuana," U.S. National Highway Traffic Safety Administration, www.nhtsa.dot.gov/people/injury/research/job185drugs/cannabis.htm

"Drug and Human Performance Fact Sheet: Cocaine," U.S. National Highway Traffic Safety Administration, www.nhtsa.dot.gov/people/injury/research/job185drugs/cocain.htm

"Drug and Human Performance Fact Sheet: Methamphetamine and Amphetamine," U.S. National Highway Traffic Safety Administration, www.nhtsa.dot.gov/people/injury/research/job185drugs/methamphetamine.htm

History of Alcohol Prohibition, www.drugtext.org/library/reports/nc/nc2a.htm

MADD Online: Minimum Age Drinking Laws, www.madd.org/stats/0,1056,4565,00.html

Tandy, Karen P., Testimony before the U.S. House of Representatives Committee on Appropriations, March 24, 2004.

## THE GALLUP ORGANIZATION

www.gallup.com

The Website of the national polling institute includes polling data and analyses on hundreds of topics.

## HISTORY OF BEER

www.beerhistory.com

Vintage television commercials and many other resources tracing the history of beer consumption in America are available on this website.

## HISTORY OF RATIONS

www.qmfound.com/history_of_rations.htm

A history of the rations provided to soldiers during wartime, which often included beer and rum, can he read on this website maintained by the Quartermaster Museum of Fort Lee, Virginia.

## MONITORING THE FUTURE

www.monitoringthefuture.org

The University of Michigan's annual report on drug use by young people can be accessed at this Internet site.

## THE CENTER ON ALCOHOL MARKETING AND YOUTH

www.camy.org

The report on the alcohol industry's use of television can be downloaded at this site maintained by the Center on Alcohol Marketing and Youth at Georgetown University.

## THIRTY YEARS OF AMERICA'S DRUG WAR

www.pbs.org/wgbh/pages/frontline/shows/drugs

Companion website to the PBS Frontline documentary *Thirty Years of America's Drug War*.

## TIMOTHY LEARY

www.lib.virginia.edu/small/exhibits/sixties/leary.html

Many resources covering the life of 1960s drug guru Timothy Leary are available on this website maintained by the University of Virginia.

## ALCOHOLICS ANONYMOUS

Grand Central Station
PO Box 459
New York, NY 10163
(212) 870-3400
Website: www.aa.org

AA members provide one another with one-to-one support to help kick their addictions. The organization, which has a membership of some 2 million, maintains more than 100,000 chapters in 150 countries.

## CENTERS FOR DISEASE CONTROL AND PREVENTION

Office of Communication
Building 16, D-42
1600 Clifton Road, N.E.
Atlanta, GA 30333
(800) 311-3435
Website: www.cdc.gov

The federal government's public health agency charts risky behavior by young people through the Youth Risk Behavior Surveillance System and has produced an abundant number of research papers on drug and alcohol abuse.

## DRUG ENFORCEMENT ADMINISTRATION

2401 Jefferson Davis Highway
Alexandria, VA 22301
(202) 307-1000
Website: www.usdoj.gov/dea

The U.S. Justice Department's chief anti-drug law enforcement agency is charged with investigating the illegal narcotics trade in the United States and helping local police agencies track down drug dealers.

## MOTHERS AGAINST DRUNK DRIVING
511 E. John Carpenter Freeway, Suite 700
Irving, TX 75062
(800) GET-MADD
Website: www.madd.org

MADD lobbies for tough laws that regulate drinking and driving and has developed many resources for the student seeking statistics and other information on the impact of driving under the influence.

## NARCOTICS ANONYMOUS
PO Box 9999
Van Nuys, CA 91409
(818) 773-9999
Website: www.na.org

The more than 20,000 chapters of Narcotics Anonymous in the United States and other countries support their members' efforts to emerge from their addictions.

## NATIONAL DRUG INTELLIGENCE CENTER
319 Washington Street, 5th Floor
Johnstown, PA 15901-1622
(814) 532-4601
Website: www.usdoj.gov/ndic

The agency produces the National Drug Threat Assessment, which identifies the primary drugs that have invaded illegal markets and tracks their availability in American communities; the report can be downloaded on the center's Internet page.

## NATIONAL INSTITUTE ON ALCOHOL ABUSE AND ALCOHOLISM
5635 Fishers Lane, MSC 9304
Bethesda, Maryland 20892-9304
(800) 662-HELP
Website: www.niaaa.nih.gov

Part of the Substance Abuse and Mental Health Services Administration, the National Institute on Alcohol Abuse and Alcoholism develops treatment and prevention programs for alcohol abuse.

## NATIONAL INSTITUTE ON DRUG ABUSE

6001 Executive Boulevard, Room 5213
Rockville, MD 20852
(301) 443-1124
Website: www.nida.nih.gov

The NIDA's mission is to help finance scientific research projects that study addiction trends.

## NATIONAL ORGANIZATION FOR REFORM OF MARIJUANA LAWS

1600 K Street NW
Suite 501
Washington, DC 20006-2832
(202) 483-5500
Website: www.norml.org

NORML lobbies for liberalization of laws governing marijuana use. The organization's report, *Crimes of Indiscretion: Marijuana Arrests in the United States*, can be downloaded at the organization's website.

## PARTNERSHIP FOR A DRUG FREE AMERICA

405 Lexington Avenue, Suite 1601
New York, NY 10174
(212) 922-1560
Website: www.drugfreeamerica.org

The Partnership has established a number of anti-drug programs as well as research projects identifying drug abuse trends in the United States.

**SUBSTANCE ABUSE AND MENTAL HEALTH SERVICES ADMINISTRATION**
1 Choke Cherry Road
Room 8-1054
Rockville, MD 20857
(240) 276-2000
Website: www.samhsa.gov

An agency of the U.S. Department of Health and Human Services, the Substance Abuse and Mental Health Services Administration issues the annual National Survey on Drug Use and Health, which can be downloaded at SAMHSA's website.

**WHITE HOUSE OFFICE OF NATIONAL DRUG CONTROL POLICY**
Drug Policy Information Clearinghouse
PO Box 6000
Rockville, MD 20849-6000
(800) 666-3332
Website: www.whitehousedrugpolicy.gov

The White House Office of National Drug Control Policy develops a national strategy to combat illegal drug use and serves as a liaison linking the different federal drug investigation and research agencies.

Numbers in ***bold italics*** refer to captions.

Page:
3: PhotoDisc
8-9: Matt Cardy/Getty Images
11: © OTTN Publishing
12: Drug Enforcement
Administration
13: Michelle Lawlor
14: © OTTN Publishing
16-17: Architect of the Capitol
19: Library of Congress
20: American Stock/Getty Images
22: Library of Congress
23: Library of Congress
26: FPG/Getty Images
27: Library of Congress
28: © OTTN Publishing
31: © OTTN Publishing
34: Library of Congress
37: both Drug Enforcement
Administration
38: Library of Congress
41: both Library of Congress
43: Michelle Lawlor
44: Drug Enforcement
Administration
45: © OTTN Publishing
47: The Richard Nixon Library &
Birthplace Foundation
49: PhotoDisc
50: both Drug Enforcement
Administration
51: © OTTN Publishing
52: both Drug Enforcement
Administration

54-55: PhotoDisc
58: Mark Wilson/Getty Images
59: Justin Sullivan/Getty Images
62: PhotoDisc
64: PhotoDisc
65: © OTTN Publishing
66: © OTTN Publishing
68: Justin Sullivan/Getty Images
71: Drug Enforcement
Administration
72: Shawn Thew/AFP/Getty Images
73: Alex Wong/Newsmakers/Getty
Images
75: © OTTN Publishing
79: Matt Cardy/Getty Images
80: © OTTN Publishing
81: © OTTN Publishing
82: Digital Vision
84: Win McNamee/Getty Images
87: Tim Boyle/Getty Images
88: (top) Ron Vesely/MLB Photos via
Getty Images; (bottom) Jason
Wise/MLB Photos via Getty
Images
89: PhotoDisc
91: Liaison/Getty Images
92: Ariel Skelley/Corbis
94: Mark Wilson/Getty Images
96: © OTTN Publishing
98: Michelle Lawlor
101: both Drug Enforcement
Administration
103: © OTTN Publishing

# CONTRIBUTORS

For almost three-quarters of a century, the **GALLUP POLL** has measured the attitudes and opinions of the American public about the major events and the most important political, social, and economic issues of the day. Founded in 1935 by Dr. George Gallup, the Gallup Poll was the world's first public opinion poll based on scientific sampling procedures. For most of its history, the Gallup Poll was sponsored by the nation's largest newspapers, which published two to four of Gallup's public opinion reports each week. Poll findings, which covered virtually every major news event and important issue facing the nation and the world, were reported in a variety of media. More recently, the poll has been conducted in partnership with CNN and USA Today. All of Gallup's findings, including many opinion trends dating back to the 1930s and 1940s, are accessible at www.gallup.com.

**ALEC M. GALLUP** is chairman of The Gallup Poll in the United States, and Chairman of The Gallup Organization Ltd. in Great Britain. He also serves as a director of The Gallup Organisation, Europe; Gallup China; and Gallup Hungary. He has been employed by Gallup since 1959 and has directed or played key roles in many of the company's most ambitious and innovative projects, including Gallup's 2002 "Survey of Nine Islamic Nations"; the "Global Cities Project"; the "Global Survey on Attitudes Towards AIDS"; the 25-nation "Health of The Planet Survey"; and the ongoing "Survey of Consumer Attitudes and Lifestyles in China." Mr. Gallup also oversees several annual "social audits," including "Black and White Relations in the United States," an investigation of attitudes and perceptions concerning the state of race relations, and "Survey of the Public's Attitudes Toward the Public Schools," which tracks attitudes on educational issues.

Mr. Gallup's educational background includes undergraduate work at Princeton University and the University of Iowa. He undertook graduate work in communications and journalism at Stanford University, and studied marketing and advertising research at New York University. His publications include *The Great American Success Story* (with George Gallup, Jr.; Dow Jones-Irwin, 1986), *Presidential Approval: A Source Book* (with George Edwards; Johns Hopkins University Press, 1990), *The Gallup Poll Cumulative Index: Public Opinion* 1935–1997 (Scholarly Resources, 1999), and *British Political Opinion 1937–2000: The Gallup Polls* (with Anthony King and Robert Wybrow; Politicos Publishing, 2001).

**HAL MARCOVITZ** has written more than seventy books for young readers. His other titles in the GALLUP MAJOR TRENDS & EVENTS series include *Technology, Abortion, Race Relations*, and *Health Care*. He lives in Chalfont, Pennsylvania, with his wife, Gail, and daughters Ashley and Michelle, and enjoys writing fiction. He is the author of the satirical novel Painting the White House.